MEGAMISTAKES

MEGAMISTAKES

Forecasting and the Myth of Rapid Technological Change

STEVEN P. SCHNAARS

THE FREE PRESS
A Division of Macmillan, Inc.
NEW YORK

Collier Macmillan Publishers
LONDON

The Free Press
A Division of Macmillan, Inc.
866 Third Avenue, New York, N.Y. 10022

Collier Macmillan Canada, Inc.

Printed in the United States of America

printing number

1 2 3 4 5 6 7 8 9 10

Library of Congress Cataloging-in-Publication Data

Schnaars, Steven P.
  Megamistakes : forecasting and the myth of rapid
technological change.

  Bibliography: p.
  Includes index.
  1. Technological forecasting. I. Title.
T174.S36   1989   658.4'01   88–21196
ISBN 0–02–927952–6

Contents

Preface

Books on forecasting tend to be either technical tomes that explain mathematical modeling or popular renditions that offer speculations on what the future will look like based on the author's view of the world. For different reasons, each type of book is of limited value when forecasting emerging new products and technologies.

The technical books offer a scholarly treatment of the subject but are written in a language and style that is inaccessible to most readers; mostly, they appeal to a small cadre of loyal model builders. More important, these books worship calculation in a chaotic world that negates the very premise of the techniques they champion. The models they propose are of especially limited value in the softer applications, such as new product and technological forecasting, where numbers are scarce and irregularities occur regularly.

Popular books on the future appeal to a wider audience. Their style makes them more readable and entertaining. But, since they usually lack the imprimatur of scholarly research and empirical support, the reader must accept the author's speculations at face value. Furthermore, those books often propose radical propositions that arise solely from speculation.

Megamistakes steers a middle course between the technical tomes and popular books on the future. It is entertaining, but it tells an important tale based on a reading of actual past forecasts. It will appeal to anyone with a curiosity about the future but is written especially for those who make present decisions that have future consequences. General managers, marketing managers, marketers, and business people of every ilk with even a passing interest in the future will benefit from its findings and enjoy its refreshing perspective.

Megamistakes examines how people in the past saw the future, and it shows how elusive accurate forecasts of emerging new products and technologies can be. There is far more than calculation involved. Many of those forecasts are hilarious in hindsight. You will ask yourself how sensible people could have said such things. I hope that you will learn to avoid similar errors in the future.

This book is not about a lot of things. If you are looking to learn the latest mathematical techniques, you will be disappointed. It contains no new models. In fact, it does not even contain any old models. Also, this is not a book about silly forecasts or rare oddball blunders but a book about common errors made by reasonable people who, like the rest of us, were caught up in the spirit of the times in which they lived. Most important, it is not an indictment of forecasting or forecasters. It is an attempt to improve on the historical record by studying the errors and successes of the past, it is not an attempt to belittle the field of forecasting. This book complements other forecasting books, it does not contradict them.

Megamistakes has its roots in the late 1970s when, as a Ph.D. student, a faculty advisor with a government grant to study solar energy asked me to look into methods that could be used to predict the percent of American homes that would adopt solar energy systems by the mid-1980s. I began to investigate market penetration models. The articles in the academic literature did not seem to be of much help for this problem. Most of them talked about technique and ignored practical applications. They seemed to assume that all you had to do was learn the required calculations to make better forecasts. There were so many things that could affect the future market for solar energy that I was suspicious of such a regimented approach to forecasting.

At about the same time, another professor asked me to review a study conducted by a prestigious consulting firm on the market penetration rates for a new and improved way of burning coal in industrial applications. The government had funded the study to the tune of a quarter of a million dollars, and his job was to find out whether it got its money's worth. The report the government received was the size of a telephone book. My job was to comment on the merits of the forecasts it contained. The report turned out to be all veneer with no solid wood. Two dozen purchasing agents were asked whether they would buy one of those systems by the 1990s. The percent that said yes was used to predict the size of the national market. Millions would be sold. I said to myself that there has to be a better way.

Starting in 1979 I began to collect examples of actual forecasts describing the emergence of major new products and exciting new technologies. Mostly, this entailed reading twenty-year-old magazines on a regular basis. I also collected reviews of past forecasts published in the business press and popular magazines. They not only were fun to read but were also instructive. I began to form ideas about why some forecasts were successful while others failed badly.

To test my impressions, in 1984 I took a probability sample of leading business magazines over a twenty-year period and searched those issues for forecasts of emerging technologies and major new products. Conrad Berenson and I published the results in an article that appeared in the Summer of 1986 issue of the *California Management Review*.

Readers responded favorably to the hits and misses described in the paper. I decided to expand the study, reexamine the forecasts in my files, and do a more thorough review. This book is the result.

I have been helped along the way by many fine people to whom I owe a great deal. Conrad Berenson, a mentor and colleague, has shaped my thoughts greatly. He has an uncanny ability to get to the heart of matters quickly. Avi Shama was the advisor who originally got me interested in forecasting. I am grateful to him for his direction, which I have followed for ten years now. Scott Armstrong, a professor at the Wharton School, has also been influential. I relied heavily on his work as a doctoral student. He has produced some of the finest work in forecasting and has also shown that research and writing can be fun as well as instructive.

I would also like to thank my wife, Gail, and my two young sons, Paul and John. My sons are convinced that an integral part of being an adult male involves sitting in front of a keyboard for extended periods and periodically calling out, "Hold on, I'll be down shortly." "Shortly" to my sons means a long time.

Finally, I would like to thank Bob Wallace, my editor at The Free Press, who has been supportive and encouraging. Working with him has been a pleasure.

STEVEN P. SCHNAARS

New York
May 1, 1988

MEGAMISTAKES

1

Introduction

Forecasting the emergence of growth markets is a perilous, but irresistible, endeavor. Some new products go on to spawn huge growth markets while others sail straight into oblivion. Consider the following pairs of products, and ask yourself why one succeeded while the other failed:

The compact disk grew quickly after its introduction in 1983, even though it required consumers to replace their record collections—usually a serious impediment to the acceptance of a new product. A decade earlier quadraphonic stereo faced a similar impediment. That innovation, however, lingered on retailers' shelves while consumers looked elsewhere for entertainment.

Sales of cellular (car) telephones grew quickly, even though the product required the coordination of more than one technology. The picture telephone, which married two existing technologies of its day—the phone and the television—failed to catch fire, even though it was pushed for decades and eventually evolved into video teleconferencing, which, in turn, failed to excite the interest of business customers.

Finally, frozen foods found a huge market as home freezers became commonplace. In fact, *Consumer Reports*, in a 1986 book titled *I'll Buy That!*, rates frozen foods as one of the fifty most prominent innovations to change our lives.[1] Dehydrated foods, however, a method tried in the 1960s, and, more recently, irradiated foods have changed our lives far less.

In hindsight, it is easy to tell the winners from the losers. At the time of their introduction, however, a bright future was

1

predicted for each of those innovations. How can the hits be distinguished from the misses beforehand?

A study of the past might help. On the following pages you will find forecasts of major new products, growth markets, emerging technologies, and significant trends that were made over the past few decades. You will discover the reasons why some of those forecasts succeeded while others failed miserably. Finally, and most important, you will gain a better understanding of how growth markets emerge and a chance to avoid repeating the errors of the past.

Looking back at the accuracy of past forecasts is not the strong suit of most forecasters. They prefer to look forward. Specifically, they prefer to develop new models and techniques for looking forward. Much of that effort proceeds in the belief that such advances lead to more accurate forecasts. It is an assumption that recent research has consistently shown to be badly mistaken. More often than not, as this book illustrates, the future sloshes forward with little regard for the regularities uncovered by those models.

Building elaborate models is especially unfruitful for the types of forecasts examined here. By definition, growth markets based on new products and technologies possess few, if any, historical data to guide us. Methodological concerns are especially impotent in such applications.

Absent from much of the methodological discussion in forecasting is a systematic examination of past forecasts. Simple questions remain unanswered: What kinds of things have led to successful forecasts in the past? What kinds of things have led to mistakes? Previous forecasts, it seems, are best forgotten or left to the criticism of a pesky outsider. They are certainly not something to dwell on. It is as if forecasters are afraid that by looking back they will be turned into the business equivalent of biblical pillars of salt.

Yet past forecasts are plentiful and potentially informative. Past mistakes may indicate common, correctable errors. Past successes may indicate the best course of action.

Actually, forecasters do look back, but often at the wrong things. Instead of focusing on how well they did in the past, they focus intently on identifying myriad past trends and patterns. For example:

• They construct elegant mathematical models, which scour past data in search of obscure patterns. Complicated patterns will regularly recur, they hope.

• They project glorious futures from the skimpiest data on the mistaken assumption that some law of upward motion applies to the evolution of new technologies. They mistakenly believe that a few years of initial sales growth portends a stunning growth market that will last for years. Often they are disappointed.

• Seers of all sorts see patterns emerging in their minds from widely scattered historical observations. We are entering an age of accelerating change, they warn. We must prepare for a future that will be far different from the past or the present.

• Others rely heavily on historical precedent. They assume that the patterns and issues of the past will persist. But in forecasting pendulums often swing in unexpected directions with wanton disregard for past trends and patterns.

Mistaken forecasts are especially fun to read, but they are also instructive. They illustrate that the same, often preventable, errors recur, even though separated by decades and contained in very different kinds of forecasts. As the cases examined in this book illustrate, those charged with looking forward often fail to learn from past mistakes. Instead, they prefer to reinvent new forecasting models that fall into the same traps as older models.

Past successes are also instructive. They indicate which aspects of the forecast should be attended to and which can be ignored.

Best of all, and contrary to the funding cries of my fellow academics, you need not gain access to a Cray computer, or even a small calculator, to implement the advice offered in this book. In fact, you would do better to stay away from both. A bit of common sense and a well-honed sense of perspective will do the trick. I am confident that forecasters armed with those meager weapons will be better suited for battle with the future than forecasters outfitted with powerful computers and impressive credentials. Battleships fight poorly in the swampy waters of forecasting.

While reading the mistakes contained in this book, you will probably ask yourself: How could reasonable people have made such outrageous mistakes? Did they really believe the future would look like that? Did large, well-managed companies actually see business opportunities in those crazy inventions? How could they have been so wrong?

It is equally likely that many of the forecasts made today will suffer a similar fate and will be subjected to similar questions in the future—even though these forecasts mimic today's widely held views of what the future will bring. To believe that today is different is to deceive yourself. There is no evidence that our capacity to foresee the future has improved at all.

But the importance of forecasting has not diminished. Innovations that spawn growth markets still provide firms with an opportunity for renewed growth and offer a fresh chance to shake free the shackles of stagnation. Mistaken forecasts—for such products as CB radios, conference TV, video telephones, and dehydrated meats—have turned into traps for unsuspecting firms. Instead of opportunities for growth, those mistaken markets have wasted time and money and distracted management from more fruitful endeavors. If innovations and growth markets are the lifeblood of industry, then mistaken forecasts are the viruses that attack that lifeblood.

Where the Forecasts Came From

The forecasts presented in this book were published in the popular business press over the last three decades. They were drawn almost exclusively from influential sources with respected reputations for excellence, credibility, and fair reporting, such as the *Wall Street Journal, Business Week, Fortune, Forbes,* the *New York Times, Newsweek,* and *Time.*

Forecasts published in those sources influenced their readers greatly, shaping readers' perceptions about the future. Furthermore, forecasts published in the popular business press often mirror the popular beliefs of the day. They reflect the views of their readers. They were not wild-eyed ideas or fringe-element opinions.

To a lesser extent, this book examines forecasts published in trade journals. Forecasts from these sources show what specific industries felt the future held for their products and markets.

Finally, popular books on the future were examined. Again,

only credible sources that would have been believed at the time the forecasts appeared were selected.

Sensational sources that published extreme forecasts were consciously avoided. *Popular Mechanics,* for example, has published many technological forecasts since at least the 1930s. But, some might argue, such forecasts are outside the mainstream and not indicative of the major trends expected by much of the populace. Sensational forecasts were not included.

The Credibility of Published Forecasts

In no way do I wish to demean the particular record of any individual forecaster, magazine, or journal. In fact, they should be commended for agreeing to accept the risk that comes with long-range forecasting. Throughout these chapters I argue that forecasting mistakes are indicative more of the times in which they were made than of the forecasters who made them. I believe that both forecasters and publishers were simply reporting on the future from the times in which they lived. They both influenced and were influenced by the dominant themes of the day.

Some might argue that forecasts published in the business press should not be taken at face value. Such critics might argue that the developments those forecasts propose are meant more for entertainment than to discern the future. Furthermore, critics might argue that in many cases advertisers, potential producers, those in search of funding or publicity, and those wishing to float trial balloons are responsible for those forecasts. You do not understand how it works, some might argue.

I vigorously disagree. First and foremost, forecasts published in the business press are published because they represent the best guesses of the day. While some posturing is surely a component of some forecasts, most forecasts are serious attempts to foresee future developments. They were widely read and widely believed by their readers.

Evaluating Forecast Accuracy

The criteria used to evaluate the forecasts in this book are strict. Simply put, forecasters were held to their own words. If, for example, a forecast called for the "widespread" use of some dazzling innovation—such as the electric car or the Wankel rotary engine—the evaluation focused on the word "widespread." Small-scale demonstration projects or other limited uses did not qualify the forecast as a success. According to this criterion, neither the electric car nor the Wankel engine has achieved widespread commercial acceptance.

Similarly, vaguely stated forecasts were eliminated, because they could not be evaluated. Forecasts that called for a decay in the quality of life, for example, or the phaseout of many chemical pesticides, could not be fairly evaluated. Whether they proved true or false depends solely on how one defines the hazy terms of the forecast.

Forecasts in the late 1960s that called for the development and use of improved "mood-altering" drugs were difficult to evaluate for the same reason. Although those forecasts were unduly influenced by the drug culture of the late 1960s and implied that large segments of the population would alter their moods regularly with psychedelic drugs, there have been many advances in psychopharmacology aimed at mental patients. To categorize such forecasts as true or false would be misleading.

Forecasts couched in contingencies were also eliminated. Forecasts that called for rapid growth of some market *if* some other event occurred first were also difficult to evaluate. So were articles in the business press that failed to take a stand and presented both sides of an issue—the opinions of those who believed a new technology would grow to dizzying heights and the opinions of those who believed the technology would go nowhere. Such articles presented the pluses and minuses of the new product. They were not forecasts.

Interestingly, forecasts published in more recent years are more likely to be couched in contingencies than forecasts from the 1960s. Ironically, even though the 1980s have proved to be a rather stable decade, the forecasts published in the business press have hedged their bets to a greater extent than forecasts from the 1960s. In a sense, practical forecasters have looked back, recognized they have been burned, and become more cautious. Unlike the 1960s, most sensible people recognize the frailty of long-range forecasts.

Finally, trivial forecasts, short-lived fads, and outright silly ideas were not included. For example, innovations like Golf-O-Tron (an early 1960s indoor multiscreen golfing simulation) or the amphibious car were not considered. Even at the time they were made they were wild ideas aimed at a small market. Clearly, such devices are not indicative of any important trends.

In sum, I tried to be fair. My *a priori* intention was not to skew the results to favor mistaken forecasts or to write a book that emphasized horrendous errors. It just turned out that way. That is what the historical record shows.

2

Overvaluations of Technological Wonder

Technological forecasting, as the name implies, is concerned with identifying new products based on innovative technologies that will produce growth markets. It is one of the most difficult kinds of forecast to make accurately. There are so many unknowns, and so many possible outcomes, that errors appear everywhere.

It is unnecessary to exaggerate the mistakes. By any sensible measure, it is easy to see that forecasters turned out to be especially poor at spotting technological trends. Even a cursory review of past forecasts reveals that most technological forecasts have been dead wrong. If fact, most technological forecasts have missed their mark not by a matter of degree, but completely, and without regard for what actually occurred years later.

The most prominent reason why technological forecasts have failed is that the people who made them have been seduced by technological wonder.

Many forecasters paint a bright future for new, emerging technologies. New technologies, they claim, will spawn huge growth markets, as the technology is used in dramatically new products. It is only the beginning, they preach. This technology will play a large part in our everyday lives.

Most of those forecasts fail because the forecasters fall in love with the technology they are based on and ignore the market the technology is intended to serve. The forecasters who construct them are blinded by their emotions and lose perspective of commonsense economic considerations. They are swept away. They incorrectly assume that consumers will find the new technology as enticing and irresistible as they do. In most instances, those assumptions are very wrong.

One of the most stunning examples of a technological forecast gone awry is TRW's "Probe." In 1966 TRW Inc. conducted a "Probe of the Future," which was widely reported on in the business press. The study sought to discover "what the world will want and need in the next 20 years."[1] It pinpointed many avenues for growth. As *Business Week* put it, "The products of the future—forecast by TRW's 'Probe' technique—hold vast opportunities for business growth."

"Probe" elicited judgmental estimates from twenty-seven top TRW scientists—a variation of the consensus-generating Delphi method. The technique is described in detail by North and Pyke in a 1969 issue of the *Harvard Business Review*.[2] "Probe" offers many advantages over other forecasting tools, the authors contended. But before rushing out to read about the technique, consider the forecasts it generated.

TRW recognized the strategic value of the forecasts it had generated and did not intend to share them with competitors. The World Future Society was allowed to view only a censored version of the TRW report.[3] Sixty-six of the 401 technological forecasts judged by experts to be "most likely to succeed" were withheld by TRW. Among the ones that were released, *nearly every prediction was wrong!* Either the forecasters were engaged in a highly sophisticated form of industrial competitive deception or they were badly mistaken.

"Probe" foresaw fantastic wonders ahead. Space travel played a prominent role in the TRW forecast. It predicted that the first manned lunar base would be established by 1977, followed by a permanent base in 1980. Also by 1980, a 500-kilowatt nuclear power plant would be operating on the moon! Getting there would be easy: By 1980 commercial passenger rockets would be operating. Finally, by 1983 a solar power plant would be placed in space, with wireless transmission back to earth.

The military would also be affected. By 1990 intelligent robot soldiers would be doing much of the fighting.

Transportation would see tremendous changes. By 1977 vertical takeoff aircraft would be used by individuals. For those still driving road-bound autos, the interstate system would be automated. By 1979, there would be automatic vehicle separation on the superhighways. Steering, braking, and speed control from a centralized substation would follow in 1990. Five years later there would be complete control, allowing drivers to "dial-a-destination." Apparently, potholes and other less exciting maintenance issues would not be a problem.

Housing would also change greatly. By the mid-1980s giant corporations would mass-produce low-cost, plastic (injection molded) modular housing. Those houses would contain many advanced features. They would have "real" air-conditioning, including germproofing. They would be not only fireproof but earthquake-, tornado-, and fallout-proof as well. Household chores would be automated. And, of course, the layout of the house would easily change with the family's needs.

Communications and education would change rapidly. Newspapers would be printed on home facsimile machines by 1978. Two years later the machines would print newspapers with information tailored to the individual's needs. By 1977 low-cost 3-D color TV for business conferences would reduce the need for business travel. Large-scale educational TV and teaching machine systems would come much sooner, by 1973.

Nuclear power had a bright future. It would supply 50 percent of the world's power by 1983. By 1984 the first fusion plant would be built.

The oceans would play an important economic role in the future. By 1981 undersea mining and farming would be common. By 1990 a nuclear-powered underwater recreation area would be in operation! Five years later there would be commercial undersea factories and motels. Was this a premonition of offshoring production?

Clearly, "Probe" failed because the forecasters were enamored of technological wonder. They ignored almost every economic aspect of the markets they sought to serve. Forecasts for undersea motels, factories, and recreation centers—nuclear powered, no less—were driven by utopian visions of wonder rather than practical realities. Even at the time, there was no economic reason to pursue those projects. In hindsight, those miscalculations appear foolish and ensured that the forecasts made from them would fail almost from the day they were made.

The most stunning observation to be made about the TRW study is not that it erred so spectacularly, but that it is remarkably typical of technological forecasts made at the time! Other forecasters foresaw many of the same events as did TRW. A review of technological forecasts from the 1960s shows that the same predictions for the same outlandish devices were made time and time again. Clearly, TRW did not exhibit clairvoyance, but it also did not perform especially poorly when compared with its contemporaries. It fared about the same. Others at the time also fell into the trap of unbridled optimism brought on by a love of exotic technology.

Forecasters fell victim to a common and correctable shortcoming: They fell in love with exotic technologies just because they were exotic and failed to consider the markets they sought to serve and the fundamental market needs they sought to satisfy with potential products derived from the technologies. The success or failure of the forecasts hinged less on the nature of the technologies themselves than it did on the practical applications to which they could be put. A key premise of forecasting is that a passionate focus on technology for its own sake spells disaster. No doubt, many of the same errors are being repeated today.

In December 1966 the *Wall Street Journal* published a series of articles on expected future developments. The forecasts covered developments in population and economic growth, farming and food production, computers, energy demand, and air transportation. The newspaper "talked to experts in many fields to get the best-informed opinions on probable developments between now and the year 2000."[4]

Ten years later, in 1976, the *Wall Street Journal* reviewed these forecasts in a second series of articles—a rare reporting of past mistakes.[5] Generally, it found its forecasts fell far wide of the mark. Still, it could not resist the temptation to try again.

More than twenty years have passed since the original forecasts were made, and more than ten years have passed since the 1976 updates. This is what the record shows.

In 1966 it was predicted that technological advances would revolutionize farming and fishing. According to one prediction:

"In the year 2000 the farmer will be a sophisticated executive with a computer for a foreman" (December 13, 1966, p. 1). An agricultural economist for International Harvester foresaw a future farm with "towers containing television scanners to keep an eye on robot tractors" (p. 1). An executive of a fertilizer producer noted: "The owner of the farm of the future will no more be out riding a tractor than the President of General Motors is out on an assembly line tightening bolts" (p. 1). Ironically, given the trend toward participatory management, that prediction proved partially correct.

The 1966 forecasts missed the run-up in farm prices in the 1970s, and the rundown in prices that followed in the 1980s. Those were the real issues of subsequent decades. Robot tractors are nowhere to be found. In fact, ordinary tractors have disappeared from many farms, auctioned off with the farm to pay for the expansion plans of farmers who believed mistaken forecasts of ever higher crop and farmland prices.

Vegetable production would also change. Sylvania Electric was working on huge indoor farms lit by fluorescent lights. Why that would be superior to farming in geographic areas that had many naturally sunny days is not explained.

Water shortages would be eliminated. Desalination of ocean water would be widely implemented to boost farm production. Massive projects like the Aswan Dam in Egypt would work wonders in undeveloped countries.

Mariculture—farming the oceans—would boost seafood production. Seaweed (with a lima bean flavor—sure to be a favorite among children) and algae offered the greatest promise. A salmon–trout hybrid, which grew at 250 times the rate of ordinary fish, would also serve as a new food. From the perspective of the engineers who were solving these problems, the hard part was over. Convincing consumers to use them was of secondary importance, at most. It was not their job.

Fish "ranches" would be common. Salmon would be raised and released to open ocean "pastures." When mature, they would instinctively return to the ranch. They would then be caught and sent to market—after being irradiated to kill microbes. Fish would be sprayed with a chemical preservative that served as an edible package. That too would simplify marketing.

Beef would be surpassed by synthetic entrées known as "analogs." Analogs are high in protein but not made of meat. General Foods was working hard on analogs. According to one executive: "Analogs can be produced to meet almost any conceivable dietary, religious, ethnic, or geographic ground rules" (p. 23). They could also be made with great efficiency—mistakenly, the primary motivator of these forecasts.

Meat would not be made obsolete by analogs, at least not right away. "Most experts agree, however, that there will be room for both meat and analogs in the years ahead" (p. 23). Swift & Co. was interested. Its research director foresaw the use of analogs in chili, stews, and processed "meafs." There were strategic implications: "But, frankly I think the analog people will find it smarter not to compete directly with meat—they could come up with food ideas we haven't even thought about" (p. 23). There is no mention of whether consumers would accept those radical food ideas.

More important, the forecasters missed the real trend in beef, which was toward less consumption of it because of perceived negative health consequences. While the industry struggled with "meafs," consumers switched to chicken and fish.

Transportation would also change dramatically. In 1966 four major aircraft developments were expected before the end of the century. The SST would start commercial service in 1971. The hypersonic transport (HST)—a 4,000-mph wonder—would begin commercial service in the early 1990s.

The HST would not make the SST obsolete. "Even with decreases in fuel and materials costs, however, HSTs are going to be extremely expensive to build and operate" (December 29, 1966, p. 13). Still, that did not deter proponents.

The Boeing 747 "jumbo jet" was scheduled to debut in 1970. It would be followed by 1,000-person vehicles derived from Lockheed's C5A military transport. Pan Am was interested. Apparently, identifying routes that required such massive capacity was of secondary importance. In the mid-1960s, technological advances took precedence over fundamental market considerations.

Finally, VSTOL—vertical or short takeoff and landing aircraft—were expected to ferry passengers between the downtown areas of large cities. Technical problems and high costs killed those planes.

Capital expenditures for new aircraft would cost plenty. Consequently, many foresaw the nationalization of the airlines. A United Airlines executive stated: "I question whether our government officials realize how close this industry is to nationalization" (April 1, 1976, p. 24). The government officials themselves must have been unaware of the trend: They deregulated the industry a few years later.

The *Wall Street Journal* writers were cautious in offering aircraft forecasts. They observed that previous forecasts had failed miserably. The prediction of the late 1940s that Americans would have personal helicopters never occurred, they noted. Still, they forged ahead.

They observed that the nuclear-powered airplane was abandoned after the government spent $1 billion on the project. The reactor shielding proved too heavy to let the plane fly efficiently. But, the *Journal* warned, the military might still be interested in the project.

Forecasts for the commercial passenger rocket never came to pass. An aerospace executive noted: "We could deliver people to far distant points in a few minutes, of course, but we doubt that civilian passengers would ever be willing to endure the discomfort of high acceleration and deceleration necessary for the trip" (December 29, 1966, p. 1). Their liability lawyers might love the prospect, however.

Radical changes in ground transportation were expected. Computer controlled highways, turbine cars, and other popular innovations turned out to be wonders of the 1960s, not subsequent decades.

The experts also predicted that at least 22 million cars would be sold in the year 2000. Ten million cars a year is a decent figure in the 1980s. There is no mention of Japanese competition, the real issue of the 1980s.

In the mid-1960s many foresaw a bright future for ultramodern mass-transit systems. There was only one problem. As one expert noted: "We can build all kinds of mass-transit vehicles, but no one has yet found what's going to make people want to get out of their cars and ride them." He raised an important point.

The *Wall Street Journal's* 1976 review of the 1966 forecasts brought a more sober view of the future of transportation. In contrast to the ebullient 1960s it noted: "Today's airline passenger or motorist should be able to step into a vehicle of the early 21st Century and feel right at home" (April 1, 1976, p. 1). Fundamental changes in both airplanes and autos would be minor. The optimism of the 1960s gave way to the temperance of the 1970s.

Computers is one of the few areas that has lived up to even the most optimistic predictions. For example, in 1956 there were 1,000 computers in the United States. By 1966 there were 30,000. RCA predicted that there would be 85,000 computers by 1975, 150,000 by 1985 and a stunning 220,000 by the end of the century—more than seventy times the current number. Computer sales were expected to grow exponentially.

In fact, computers sales grew even faster. With the advent of personal computers in the early 1980s, millions of computers were sold every year, not just hundreds of thousands. Computer forecasts are exceptional in this regard. It is one of very few industries where optimism was warranted.

Forecasts of how computers would affect business were much less accurate. A popular belief was that computers would cut paper work dramatically. Electronic banking would be pervasive. Instead, progress has been slower than expected, even though the technology has existed for years. Checking accounts are still widespread—consumers prefer to "play the float," and paper records are still common.

Even famous futurists can be seduced by technological wonder; in fact, it is often the currency they trade in. In 1967, the late Herman Kahn, the optimistic director of the Hudson Institute—a well-known future-oriented organization—published (with Anthony Wiener) a popular book on the future, *The Year 2000*. The cover states its purpose: "This book projects what our own world most probably will be like a generation from now." The authors offer "One Hundred Technical Innovations Very Likely in the Last Third of the Twentieth Century."[6] The dramatic developments it foresaw are listed in Table 2-1.

Companies listened attentively to those likely trends. In 1967, at a private seminar sponsored by Union Carbide, Reynolds Metals, Continental Oil, and American Smelting & Refining, Kahn disclosed the "most likely" discoveries in store for America.[7]

TABLE 2-1. Kahn and Wiener's One Hundred Technical Innovations Very Likely in the Last Third of the Twentieth Century

1. Multiple applications for lasers and masers for sensing, measuring, communication, cutting, welding, power transmission, illumination, and destructive (defensive)
2. Extreme high-strength and/or high-temperature structural materials
3. New or improved superperformance fabrics (papers, fibers, and plastics)
4. New or improved materials for equipment and appliances
5. New airborne vehicles (ground-effect machines, VSTOL and STOL, superhelicopters, giant and/or supersonic jets)
6. Extensive commercial application of shape-charge explosives
7. More reliable and long-range weather forecasting
8. Expansion of tropical agriculture and forestry
9. New sources of power for fixed installations (e.g., magnetohydrodynamic, thermionic, thermoelectric, and radioactivity)
10. New sources of power for ground transportation (storage battery, fuel cell, electromagnetic fields, jet engine)
11. Extensive use of high-altitude cameras for mapping, prospecting, census, and geological investigations)
12. New methods of water transportation (large submarines, flexible container ships, automated single-purpose bulk cargo ships)
13. Major reduction in hereditary and congenital defects
14. Extensive use of cyborg techniques (mechanical substitutes for human organs, senses, limbs)
15. New techniques for preserving and improving the environment
16. Relative effective appetite control
17. New techniques and institutions for adult education
18. New and useful plant and animal species
19. Human hibernation for short periods (hours or days)
20. Inexpensive design and procurement of "one of a kind" items through the use of computerized analysis and automated production
21. Controlled and/or supereffective relaxation and sleep
22. More sophisticated architectural engineering (geodesic domes, "fancy" stressed shells, pressurized skins, and esoteric materials)
23. New and improved uses of the oceans (mining, farming, energy)
24. Three-dimensional photography, illustrations, movies, and television
25. Automated or more mechanized housekeeping and home maintenance
26. Widespread use of nuclear reactors for power
27. The use of nuclear explosives for excavation and mining, generation of power, creation of high-temperature-pressure environments, or as a source of neutrons or other radiation
28. General use of automation and cybernation in management and production

TABLE 2-1 (continued)

29. Extensive and intensive centralization (or automatic interconnection) of current and past personal and business information in high-speed data processors
30. New and possibly pervasive techniques for surveillance, monitoring, and control of individuals and organizations
31. Some control of weather and/or climate
32. Changes or experiments with the overall environment (increase in C-14, carbon dioxide)
33. New and more reliable "educational" and propaganda techniques for affecting human behavior—public and private
34. Practical use of direct electronic communication with and stimulation of the brain
35. Human hibernation for relatively extensive periods (months to years)
36. Cheap and widely available central weapon systems
37. New and relatively effective counterinsurgency techniques (and perhaps also insurgency techniques)
38. New techniques for very cheap, convenient, and reliable birth control
39. New, more varied, and more reliable drugs for control of fatigue, relaxation, alertness, mood, personality, perceptions, fantasies, and other psychobiological states
40. Capability to choose the sex of unborn children
41. Improved capability to "change" sex of children or adults
42. Genetic control or influence over the "basic constitution" of an individual
43. New techniques and institutions for the education of children
44. General and substantial increase in life expectancy, postponement of aging, and limited rejuvenation
45. Generally acceptable and competitive synthetic foods and beverages
46. "High quality" medical care for underdeveloped areas
47. Design and extensive use of responsive and supercontrolled environments for private and public use (for pleasurable, educational, and vocational purposes)
48. Physically nonharmful methods of overindulging
49. Simple techniques for extensive and "permanent" cosmetological changes (features, "figures," perhaps complexion and even skin color)
50. More extensive use of transplantation of human organs
51. Permanent manned satellite and lunar installations—interplanetary travel
52. Application of space life systems or similar techniques to terrestrial installations
53. Permanent inhabited undersea installations and colonies
54. Automated grocery and department stores
55. Extensive use of robots and machines "slaved" to humans

TABLE 2-1 (continued)

56. New use of underground "tunnels" for private and public transportation and other purposes
57. Automated universal (real-time) credit, audit and banking systems
58. Chemical methods for improving memory and learning
59. Greater use of underground buildings
60. New and improved materials and equipment for buildings and interiors (e.g., variable transmission glass, heating and cooling by thermoelectric effect, and electroluminescent and phosphorescent lighting)
61. Widespread use of cryogenics
62. Improved chemical control of some mental illnesses and some aspects of senility
63. Mechanical and chemical methods for improving human analytical ability
64. Inexpensive and rapid techniques for making tunnels
65. Major improvements in earthmoving and construction equipment
66. New techniques for keeping physically fit and/or acquiring physical skills
67. Commercial extraction of oil from shale
68. Recoverable boosters for economic space launching
69. Individual flying platforms
70. Simple inexpensive home video recording and playing
71. Inexpensive high-capacity, worldwide, regional, and local (home and business) communication (perhaps using satellites, lasers, and light pipes)
72. Practical home and business use of "wired" video communication for both telephone and TV (possibly including retrieval of taped material from libraries) and rapid transmission and reception of facsimile
73. Practical large-scale desalination
74. Pervasive business use of computers
75. Shared time (public and interconnected?) computers available to home and business on a metered basis
76. Other widespread use of computers for intellectual and professional assistance (translation, traffic control, literature search, design and analysis)
77. General availability of inexpensive transuranic and other esoteric elements
78. Space defense systems
79. Inexpensive and reasonably effective ground-based BMD
80. Very low-cost buildings for home and business use
81. Personal "pagers" (perhaps even two-way pocket phones)
82. Direct broadcasts from satellites to home receivers
83. Inexpensive (less than $20), long-lasting, very small battery-operated TV receivers

TABLE 2-1 (continued)

---

84. Home computers to "run" household and communicate with outside world
85. Maintenance-free, longlife electronic equipment
86. Home education via video, computerized, and programmed learning
87. Stimulated, planned, and perhaps programmed dreams
88. Inexpensive, rapid, high-quality reproduction; followed by color and high-detailed photography reproduction—perhaps for home as well as office use
89. Widespread use of improved fluid amplifiers
90. Conference TV
91. Flexible penology without necessarily using prisons (by use of modern methods of surveillance, monitoring, and control
92. Common use of individual power source for lights, appliances, and machines
93. Inexpensive worldwide transportation of humans and cargo
94. Inexpensive road-free (and facility-free) transportation
95. New methods for rapid language teaching
96. Extensive genetic control for plants and animals
97. New biological and chemical methods to identify, trace, incapacitate, or annoy people for police and military uses
98. New and possibly very simple methods for lethal biological and chemical warfare
99. Artificial moons and other methods for illuminating large areas at night
100. Extensive use of "biological processes" in the extraction and processing of minerals

---

SOURCE: Reprinted with permission of Macmillan Publishing Company from *The Year 2000: A Framework for Speculation on the Next Thirty-Three Years*, pp. 51–55, by Herman Kahn and Anthony J. Wiener. Copyright © 1967 by the Hudson Institute, Inc.

Today, those companies face a much changed world. Unfortunately, this study did not prepare them for it.

Using any sensible tally, the overall record of accuracy for the Kahn and Wiener forecasts is dismal. Only about 15 percent of the forecasts clearly proved correct—or look as though they will prove correct in the final decade of the century. Another 10 percent can be judged as partially correct if a more lenient yardstick is used to measure accuracy and if the most beneficial interpretation is given to the forecasts.

Almost half of the forecasts were outright, clear-cut mistakes. They included forecasts that called for synthetic foods and beverages, extensive control of the weather, ocean mining and farming, 3-D photography, and even a method that would let people decide what they want to dream about before they go to sleep. Also, artificial "moons" that would provide light for large areas at night never came to pass.

Kahn and Wiener expected medical advances to be breathtaking. Life spans would increase, aging would be postponed, and persons would "hibernate" for months at a time. There would also be extensive use of cyborg (joining man to machine) techniques and cryogenics (deep-freezing humans). There would be direct communication with the brain. Appetites would be controlled, and there would be physically nonharmful methods of overindulging.

Education would be revolutionized. There would be extensive use of programmed learning, as well as mechanical and chemical methods for improving human analytical ability. But, many of those communication innovations would lead to propaganda devices. We must be careful, Kahn warned at the seminar.

Cars would also be changing quickly. They would be powered by jets and turbines, and electric vehicles would be widely available. Individual flying platforms would be used as an alternative to "road-bound" vehicles.

Many of us would be living in odd places, according to this study. There would be permanent manned satellite and lunar installations, along with interplanetary travel. Permanent inhabited undersea colonies would be operating, and there would be greater use of underground buildings. Meanwhile, people continue to live on the surface of this planet exclusively, in houses made of sticks, bricks, or stones.

Household chores would be automated, with extensive use of robots and machines "slaved" to humans. It is difficult to envision exactly what the forecasters had in mind with this prediction, but it is clear that they were expecting something more than a microwave oven.

Kahn echoed the often stated refrain that we live in a world that is changing rapidly. He cautioned his audience: "All these predictions assume that present rates of innovation will continue. In a rapidly changing world, *this is the only basis for predictions*" (p. 113; emphasis added).

It was not, and it was wrong. The go-go years of the 1960s

quickly gave way to the recession-plagued 1970s, which themselves gave way to the economic growth of the mid-1980s. The dominant issues of the 1960s, 1970s, and 1980s were all very different. The race for space in the 1960s, and the technological developments that accompanied it, did not continue into the 1970s; the trend ended abruptly with the decade. The energy crises of the 1970s refocused our attention. We thought about energy in the 1970s and forgot about space. We forgot about both in the 1980s.

None of the predictions foresaw the real issues of the next two decades. There was no mention of the energy problems that characterized the 1970s. Nor was there any mention of trade imbalances and the success of Japanese imports (although Kahn did write a book on the topic in 1979—twelve years after the forecasts were offered). Space travel and exotic, cost-be-damned innovations were at the forefront in the 1960s.

The oceans, which were often the focus of forecasts in the 1960s, turned out to be a valuable resource in the 1980s, but not in a way anticipated in the 1960s. We still do not engage in extensive ocean mining and farming, and undersea hotels seem comical in hindsight. Today, however, people like to eat more fish because it is more healthful. Sales have boomed. Such is the way in which long-range forecasts come to fruition. Few enter through the front door. Most sneak in through the back somehow.

Roughly 25 percent of the forecasts in *The Year 2000* could not be evaluated because they were stated vaguely and could be judged successes or failures depending on how the terms of the forecasts were defined. For example, forecasts that called for new or improved materials for equipment and appliances, or improved chemical control of some mental illnesses and some aspects of senility, could not fairly be listed as "hits" or "misses." Appliances today are more efficient, but they are not radically different. Chemical therapies have improved mental illness, but they have not eliminated it.

Mostly, forecasts containing the modifiers "effective," "improved," and other difficult to evaluate terms were judged too hazy to classify. Then, as now, these terms are too soft in meaning to pin down.

Only about 15 percent of the forecasts in the *The Year 2000* were clearly correct. Kahn and Wiener foresaw the emergence of the pocket-sized (personal) television, the VCR, and the personal pager—three clear hits. They also foresaw the tremendous influence of computers on business and banking for data collection, and for professional and personal uses. They were also correct in their predictions for satellite communications and high-altitude photography for geological surveys.

The final 10 percent of the forecasts could be judged correct in at least some instances. For example, Kahn foresaw automated grocery and department stores. Although department stores have not automated, and supermarkets are not totally automated, the rise of scanners in some stores qualifies as a partial hit.

Similarly, automation has made inroads in some production facilities, but not management tasks. Other calls, such as the one for the production of "one of a kind" items, may have worked for Cabbage Patch dolls and other limited items, but the practice is not widespread and certainly does not characterize standard production practices. Finally, such developments as conference TV, space defense systems, and monitoring and controlling prisoners with electronics rather than prisons have moved slowly toward fruition.

Some might argue that the forecasts presented in *The Year 2000* were intended less to enlighten than to amuse. Others might say that they were extreme forecasts believed only by a few, even at the time they were made. The results of an opinion poll the following year refute both contentions.

In May 1968 *Industrial Research* reported on the results of an opinion poll of 1,433 scientists and engineers.[8] The experts were asked to estimate when, if ever, each of the hundred innovations predicted by Kahn and Wiener would be realized. Their responses were placed into four categories: innovations that were expected to occur (1) before 1975, (2) between 1975 and 2000, (3) after 2000, and (4) never. Innovations were placed in the category that most experts picked.

The experts' evaluations largely mirrored Kahn and Wiener's forecasts.

Only eight developments were picked to occur before 1975—a seven-year time horizon. In hindsight, less than half of those innovations were ever successful. The experts correctly foresaw tremendous growth in the business use of computers and simple, inexpensive home video recording, two clear hits. They came close with a forecast for extensive transplantation of human organs. But they missed on many of the same forecasts as other studies—reliable long-range weather forecasts and "new" methods of education (yet another call for programmed learning).

The largest number of innovations were expected in the last quarter of the century—after 1975, but before 2000. This list contained many arcane predictions, such as individual flying platforms, the picture telephone, and moving sidewalks for local transportation, which, clearly, did not occur. By far, most of the forecasts in this group were mistaken.

Many other innovations were expected to occur after the year 2000. They included forecasts for long-term human hibernation, commercial passenger rockets, and large-scale lunar colonies. The optimism of those forecasters is captured by the fact that only four of the hundred innovations were expected never to occur: (1) physically nonharmful ways to overindulge, (2) "true" artificial intelligence, (3) modification of the solar system, and (4) major modifications of the human species (no longer *Homo sapiens*).

In the opinion poll, as well as in the Kahn study, there were no instances where a development came true before the experts said it would. Clearly, errors were on the side of optimism. In the go-go years of the late-1960s, after a decade of almost uninterrupted economic growth and the placing of a man on the moon, even the craziest, most economically nonsensical ideas seemed likely to occur.

Relying on large groups of distinguished experts also did not seem to improve accuracy. In 1969, *Industrial Research* conducted an opinion poll of research directors at most major industrial corporations to see what developments would occur within the next ten years. The poll was supplemented by "our distinguished Editorial Advisory Board."[9]

A ten-year time horizon was selected, because "10 years is a manageable time span. Developments of the next decade will be based pretty much on today's research." God help us!

As Table 2–2 illustrates, the experts saw plastic buildings, nuclear-powered aircraft, holographic 3-D movies and television, 150- to 200-year human life spans, workable nuclear fusion,

TABLE 2-2. Looking Forward: 10 Years Ahead

1. Plastics as primary structures in buildings
2. Manned exploration of Mars and Venus
3. Room temperature superconducting materials
4. Use of superconducting coils for levitating speed vehicles; superconducting power lines
5. Ultrahigh-speed ground transportation
6. Superhigh-speed submersibles
7. Adhesive-bonded aircraft
8. Nuclear-powered aircraft
9. Fast breeder reactors for power generation
10. Sustained nuclear fusion to produce power
11. Practical high-energy density batteries
12. Holographic 3-D movies and television
13. Extensive use of robots and machines "slaved" to humans
14. Cancer cure or prevention
15. 150- to 200-year human life spans
16. Automatic long-term birth control
17. Chemical–biological weapons race
18. Creation of artificial life
19. Wide use of forest fertilization
20. Mind-expanding/mood-regulating drugs to combat mental illness
21. Elimination of organ rejection in transplants
22. Low-cost solid-state TV receivers

manned exploration of Mars and Venus, and levitating high-speed vehicles—among other wonders, almost none of which came to pass.

Of the twenty-two technological forecasts in the study, only one—low-cost, solid-state TV receivers—could be judged categorically as a success. Another, elimination of organ transplant rejection, comes close. Two others—mind-expanding and mood-regulating drugs for combating mental illness, and the widespread use of forest fertilization—were difficult to categorize. Still, their percentage of "hits" is dismal, less than 20 percent by any sensible measure.

In 1967 *Fortune* presented a series of articles titled "The U.S. Economy in a New Era."[10] The articles looked at the future of the economy, housing, the automobile, population trends and home goods. The series was one of the most comprehensive examinations of the future published in the business press at the time. It was certainly one of the longest.

The series was preceded in January 1967 by a report that examined "Where the Industries of the Seventies Will Come From."[11] It began by eschewing the pessimism of earlier forecasts and arguing that we are in the midst of a great transition. We have entered a new age, the author claimed. The driving force of the new age is the chemical-electronic-aerospace complex, a variation on the military-industrial complex.

According to this forecast, two key events would push back the frontiers of technological development: (1) the growth in government-funded research and development and (2) systems management. GE, for example, used systems analysis in 1957 to estimate how long-distance nuclear ocean freighters would affect the shipping industry. It could have used a crystal ball. The method did not matter. Asking the right questions did. Nuclear ships had no effect on the industry. Lower-cost international competitors did.

The article looked at where existing technologies would head in the 1970s. Transistors would lead to integrated circuits, which in turn would lead to miniaturization of existing products. That occurred exactly as predicted.

The forecast also foresaw widespread uses for the jet engine. Vertical or short takeoff and landing (VSTOL), jumbo jets, and supersonic transports were about to create a revolution in air transport. Only jumbo jets made it.

Television would not stop with color. The industry would be reshaped by worldwide satellite communications. Not bad. That is precisely the direction in which the industry moved.

Finally, atomic power and space science would continue to emerge as profitable economic enterprises. Neither did.

The article then looked at some specific technologies that would create new industries in the 1970s. Lasers were highest on the list. They would be used in large-screen TVs and computer display screens. Three-D television was coming, as was 3-D photography, better known as holography. Cancer surgery and tunnel-boring machines were other applications.

Lasers have found practical uses in surgery, but TV pictures are still projected the old-fashioned way, in only two dimensions; 3-D is amusing, but it has served no need.

Superconductivity would also create a new industry in the 1970s. Supercooled cables would transmit electricity without the leakage found in existing cables. It would also lead to more powerful electromagnets, which could be used to harness the power of nuclear fusion. Undersea transportation, through the force of superconductive magnetic fields, would also be practical. Superconductors could be a billion-dollar industry by the mid-1970s.

Superconductors have yet to make it out of the lab, and it is still unclear when, if ever, practical products will appear. But twenty years later, the same predictions still abound. A 1987 *Business Week* article titled "The New World of Superconductivity" recycles some very old forecasts. Superconductors will lead to more efficient electricity transmission, levitating trains, supercooled microchips, and nuclear fusion. We are entering what one expert calls, "the third age of electronics."[12] In a related article titled "Our Life Has Changed," the magazine talks of a "cold" rush.[13] But, the 1987 forecasts are unquestionably more tempered than their predecessors. The magazine warns that it will take twenty years for practical products to emerge.

Energy-saving devices would also spawn new industries, according to the 1967 *Fortune* article. Rechargeable batteries, solar cells, atomic batteries, fuel cells, and other exotic devices cost much more than more traditional power sources but would soon find uses in consumer markets as costs dropped drastically. Autos powered by fuel cells were a likely starting point. Thermoelectric refrigerators and air conditioners, where motors, compressors, and fans are replaced by the direct conversion of electricity to heating or cooling, would be another emerging market. A cordless revolution in domestic appliances was also expected. Advances in rechargeable batteries would eliminate the need for pesky power cords. No more tripping over power cords in the 1970s. Typewriters, tools, tractors, and all sorts of personal electronic products would be unplugged. Small cordless domestic robots would be available by the end of the decade.

Most of those devices never made it to market. Some cordless appliances are available, the mini-vacuum cleaner for example, but we still live in a world that plugs products into sockets.

The motivation for those forecasts was not to save energy in the face of the impending energy crises of the 1970s—the forecast is not that prescient—but to save power on space vehicles and manned space flights, which was a growth market itself. The forecasters were looking in the right direction, but for the wrong reason. Chance was as important as foresight.

The materials used to make products would cause a revolution. One material, introduced in 1964, would lead the way into the 1970s. The product was Corfam, an artificial leather. Correctly, the article predicted: "Corfam is showing signs of being the bellwether of a new multi-billion dollar business in the next decade that may transform the whole shoe and leatherworking industry."[14] Corfam was a bellwether, but not in the way expected. Corfam went on to become one of the biggest-ever marketing failures. The shoe industry declined as precipitously as Corfam as production moved overseas. Shoes are still made of leather, but they are made elsewhere. The rise in athletic footwear, which relies on nylon, proved to be the only potent substitute for leather.

The article also looked at the future of older industries. Gas turbine engines would speed up trains to over 100 mph. Air-cushioned trains traveling in tubes would reach over 300 mph. Studies into improved tunneling techniques were under way. Bring on the laser tunneling devices.

Sea transportation would also change greatly by the 1970s. The development of fast nuclear merchant ships would save the industry. Hovercraft and hydrofoils would help. Nothing helped. In fact, those designs probably distracted people in the industry from the real issue they faced: cheaper international competition. There is no technological fix for U.S. shipping.

Housing construction and publishing were industries based on "ancient handicrafts." Modern methods would bring them into the 1970s. New cities of 100,000 to 200,000 would be built from scratch. Computers would change the way in which newspapers and books were published.

Building methods changed little in the 1970s or 1980s. Publishing, however, has adopted computer technology with enthusiasm. Newspapers are now widely produced using modern methods. Stories are composed, edited, and integrated electronically. Why one industry and not the other? Words, the raw material of publishing, are far more amenable to computerization than construction materials.

A related forecast foresaw an emerging market for electronic data bases. Lockheed, which in 1964 started to pursue information storage and retrieval systems, had some initial success. Its system evolved into Dialog, which abstracts articles for researchers. The market has proved one of the bright spots in information services.

Preposterous technological forecasts were not restricted to the 1960s, although during that decade there was an undeniable inclination toward ridiculous forecasts. In 1981 *Business Week* stepped up to bat and looked ahead at the coming decade in a cover story titled "Technologies for the 1980s." Its analysis saw wonders aplenty in the years ahead. The availability of venture capital and a renewed commitment to research and development would lead to "startling" new technologies that, in turn, would lead to practical new products by the end of the decade. The article announced that "this new technology could have a more profound effect on the way people live than the invention of the electric light, the radio, or the airplane."[15] Score strike one for calling for big changes in the way we lead our lives. An examination of similar forecasts made over the previous two decades would have indicated that such statements are doomed to turn out overly optimistic.

In addition, those forecasters believed that the technologies would lead to "big payoffs." Strike two for trying to cull the moderate to mediocre successes from those few long hits. An examination of past forecasts would also have revealed that predicting innovations that lead to big payoffs is an impossible task.

The strikeout occurs when the forecasters call for the changes to occur at "breathtaking speeds." Real changes almost always occur more slowly. As a result, this attempt at technological forecasting performed about as well as forecasts made in the 1960s. Most of the predictions it made never came to pass.

The forecasts are clustered into six key areas: electronics, artificial intelligence, materials, surfaces, biotechnology, and geology.

Changes in electronics would be "astonishing." By the latter half of the 1980s Josephson junctions would be commercialized. There was only one problem—the devices require cryogenic cooling. Not to worry. The problem would be licked by the end of the decade. One possibility was to put the supercomputers in space orbit and beam the information back to earth. That innovation, along with gallium-arsenide chips, would serve only niche markets, it was warned. The reason? Both were much more expensive than existing silicon technology. In reality, those severe disadvantages meant that there was no market for the products. They never replaced silicon technology. IBM killed work on Josephson junctions in 1983, two years after the forecast.

Optical computers, some believed, would ultimately replace silicon. Optical fibers were considered the next logical step toward the photonic age. So far it has not happened. It is good advice to be skeptical of any forecast that calls for a new age.

Other forecasts held that artificial intelligence (AI) would change the conditions of human life greatly. Advances in AI would "have the most sweeping implications for business and society of any technology yet devised, eclipsing even the enormous changes already wrought by computers" (p. 50). Forecasting that an industry will move faster than computers, which, in hindsight, has proved to be a remarkable and unique example of sustained market growth, is risky. It is also likely to be badly mistaken. In fact, such stunning forecasts for AI have proved to be far too optimistic. For example, experts called for the emergence of entire new industries based on "knowledge engineering." Superintelligent computers would explore problems beyond the scope of mere humans. "Mind amplifiers" would allow professionals to talk back and forth with computers to answer perplexing problems.

AI would lead to big changes on the factory floor. Robots would be hooked into elaborate production systems that made their own decisions. By the late-1980s household robots, made possible by AI, would not only perform housework but would be able to fix appliances as well.

There was a warning that these predictions would be overly optimistic, but it was not heeded. The article noted that AI had suffered from excessive promises in the 1950s. But by the 1980s times had changed greatly. Things were now different. As one expert noted, "a whole new explosion" was under way. Instead, these forecasts blew up in their makers' faces. Every one of them turned out to be way ahead of its time and, possibly, any time.

Another explosion would be occurring in materials and surfaces technology. Ceramics would soon conduct electricity and be forged like metals. Alcoa was hurling molten aluminum at cryogenically cooled surfaces to reduce corrosion and increase strength. The market for graphite fibers would explode. Super batteries and organic conductors would be available.

Forecasts for biotechnology were more realistic, but optimism ruled in those forecasts as well. There was talk of a market for human growth hormone, a clear hit. But there was also talk of designing animals to specifications, as well as producing new species of animals. Except in the kindest interpretation of events, those forecasts proved extreme.

Geology would be rocked by satellites, computers, and artificial intelligence. Combinations of technologies would greatly improve the ability to locate resources. Not bad. There have been advances in those areas. What the technologies would not affect, and what the forecasts failed to foresee, was that the energy and minerals business collapsed.

These forecasts committed the exact same errors as those made in the 1960s. Had the forecasters who made them reviewed the errors of the past, I am certain they would have toned down their predictions and would have been closer to the actual outcomes.

In 1980 *Business Week* looked ahead to the year 2000 at "The Coming Impact of Microelectronics."[16] By 1985, it predicted, autos would use microelectronic chips to boost efficiency. Ten percent of homes would have computers or terminals. Not bad. Two clear hits, even though part of the prediction was that the computers would be connected to remote data bases by, among other things, a two-way cable.

The record fades as the time horizon of the forecasts lengthens. By 1990 microelectronics would be controlling artificial hearts and other human organs. Most doctors would rely on computer-aided diagnostic equipment. Robots would begin to hurt factory employment. In hindsight, international competition hurt much worse. Autos, it was predicted, would have microcomputers to signal when maintenance was due and to diagnose problems. Banks would be interconnected by computer networks. A total of three misses and two close calls.

More wondrous devices would appear by the year 2000.

"Smart" highways would automate driving. There would be home medicine via computers. Robots, driven by microelectronics, would cause extensive dislodgment of the labor force.

Even dentistry foresaw technological wonders. In 1968, the Director of the National Institute of Dental Research, a division of the U.S. Public Health Service, predicted that "in the next decade, both tooth decay and the most prevalent form of gum disease will come to a virtual end."[17] According to experts at that agency, by the late 1970s false teeth and dentures would be 'anachronisms," replaced by plastic tooth implant technology. A vaccine against tooth decay would also be widely available, and there would be little need for dental drilling.

Many of the predictions covered in this chapter are outlandish, but they are certainly not new. Isaac Asimov, in a cute little book titled *Futuredays*, looks at a series of illustrations drawn by a French commercial artist in 1899.[18] The illustrations depicted a vision of life in the year 2000. According to this view, there would be submarine ocean liners, pills for dinner instead of food, automated learning in the schools, home robots, automated farming, extensive use of the ocean bottoms for business and entertainment, and the widespread use of nuclear energy, including home heating with radium burning in the fireplace. Three-quarters of a century later, many forecasts were still calling for the same events. The style of their predictions had changed but the underlying substance remained pretty much the same.

The technological forecasts examined in this chapter suggest that only 20 to 25 percent of such forecasts come true. The rest are either grossly mistaken or cannot be classified.

Previous studies of the accuracy of technological forecasts are rare and paint a prettier picture than really exists. Wise, in a 1976 issue of *Futures*, for example, examined 1,556 technological forecasts made between 1890 and 1940 and concluded that about 60 percent of the forecasts were mistaken.[19] He also found that expert forecasters were no more accurate than nonexperts, a finding now common to all kinds of forecasts.

Wise confronts the findings of Gilfillian, who conducted a similar study in 1937 and found that expert forecasts of new technologies were correct about 66 percent of the time.[20] Wise implies that Gilfillian had stacked the deck.

A study I conducted with Conrad Berenson, published in *Cali-*

fornia Management Review in 1986, found results similar to Wise's.[21] About half of the predictions of growth markets published in the popular business press since 1960 were mistaken.

Still, simple nose-counting of the hits and misses is misleading. A closer examination reveals that the record is far worse than the numbers suggest. The magnitude of the mistakes, outdated data, and double-counting of successes suggest that the 20 to 25 percent figure presented above is probably more accurate.

It is clear that technological forecasting is an irresistible but risky endeavor. It is fun to speculate on the nature of innovations that will pervade our lives in the future. Unfortunately, the success of such speculation has been less than encouraging. There is almost no evidence that forecasters, professionals and amateurs alike, have any idea what our technological future will look like. After reading the forecasts examined in this chapter, the most sensible conclusion about technological forecasting is drawn by *Time* magazine: "The seeds of tomorrow are buried in today. But, they lie much too deep, and germinate much too subtly, for ordinary eyes—or even computers—to detect all of their potential fruits."[22]

3

Life at Home in the Future

O ver the years, forecasters have sought to foresee what every-day life would be like in the years ahead. In past decades the home of the future has taken many forms, each view dominated by the spirit of the times, but largely unrelated to the ultimate outcome. Each time, it was widely believed that technology would play a prominent role in our future lives.

In the 1960s forecasters foresaw a home replete with fantastic inventions that would ease the burden of tedious household chores. The home of the future, when viewed from the 1960s, was about to change greatly as space technology filtered down to everyday uses. Forecasts made during the 1970s, in contrast, foresaw a home replete with energy-saving devices that would also change our lives greatly, but this time with a different set of inventions, to accomplish a different set of goals.

In the 1960s many believed that the home itself would change dramatically. Modern production techniques would revolutionize home building as it had auto building. The analogy was clear. Housing too would move from the old craftsmans' model of on-site construction of individual units to low-cost, mass-produced modular housing. It was not a new idea. Since the 1930s fore-casters have foreseen the emergence of modular housing.

The procedure would work as follows: A temporary factory would be set up on the building site to produce, using assembly-line techniques, standardized dwelling modules. Cranes would stack the modules, and workers would fasten them in place. Larger apartments would consist of more individual modules than smaller apartments.

The primary appeal of modular housing was its lower cost. Furthermore, the system would help house the poor. Low-cost housing would be available to all.

The idea culminated with the building of Habitat, a 158-unit project at the Montreal Expo 67. That project signaled the beginning of a bright future for modular housing.

Modular housing never made it. The *New York Times* analyzed the case for modular housing twenty years after the building of Habitat. It discovered that the project had not been copied elsewhere.

Lower costs never materialized. "It was just always easier and cheaper to build conventionally," the article noted.[1] Furthermore, land is the single most expensive item in building, and its cost is not affected by modular techniques. Also, conventional building techniques have become more productive. Even the cost of Habitat should have aroused suspicions. In 1967 it cost $85,500 to construct a single Habitat unit. At the time, similar apartments in Montreal were selling for $13,000, and entire houses were selling for $20,000. Those inflated costs were attributed to a project smaller than expected and the fact that it was for a world's fair.

Modular housing seemed not to help urban renewal projects either. Large-scale housing projects hastened the decline of entire neighborhoods by pulling huge numbers of residents into the projects. In the 1980s we are demolishing the projects to make room for lower-density housing.

Still, in 1987 the architect of Habitat remains confident: "That it didn't succeed does not mean that it won't happen. It won't be a revolution as I thought, but an evolution." For the foreseeable future, extinction seems to be the more appropriate Darwinian analogy.

In 1967 the *Wall Street Journal* again looked at the future in a series titled "Shape of the Future."[2] An article by Herbert Lawson looked at the home of the future. It relied heavily on the expectations of researchers and designers at Philco-Ford, a Ford Motor subsidiary. According to those experts, tomorrow's dwellings would be "a 'great adventure' in living" (p. 1). Factory-made housing would eliminate the need for most on-site building. "Building houses by hand as we do is ludicrous," one expert noted (p. 13). Others were less optimistic and, consequently, more correct. Monsanto, which built a plastic house of the future, recognized that high costs would stall penetration of radical designs. One executive noted: "I'd guess that 30 years from now there will still be a lot of Cape Cods built" (p. 13). Still, most experts agreed that factory-built components would make significant inroads in housing.

The future was shaped with household appliances that would perform new and radical functions. According to Philco experts, electrostatic air filters and ultrasonic cleaners would be installed just inside home entrances to remove dust from the clothes of those entering the home. Shoes would be cleaned by vibrating floor grills also placed at entrances. Dishes would be disposable. A dish-molding machine would manufacture new dishes for every meal. The process would be so cheap that bowls, plates, and cups would be obsolete.

Experts at General Electric were expecting radical changes in the ways we handle household garbage. Within a few decades household devices based on lasers would vaporize garbage. Today we still simply dump our trash, although I would not be surprised if Strategic Defense Initiative proponents resurrect the household laser garbage handler as a feasible by-product of their program.

The microwave oven would soon populate household kitchens as prices dropped. Both Philco and GE were looking a step ahead. They were combining the microwave with the freezer. With integrated circuits it would soon be possible for housewives to press a few buttons and automatically transfer frozen foods into cooked delights. The combination device never made it to market.

Like many other forecasts of the day, the video recorder was expected to grow briskly once costs fell. The study went a step further. It foresaw the sale and rental of video tapes by stores and libraries. That is precisely the way the market has evolved.

Forecasts about television were less prescient. In step with other studies at the time, this study predicted that the next logical step in the progression of TV was a tie-in with holography. Soon, TV would be 3-D. With the exception of second-rate movie gimmicks, it never happened.

One of the most comical, yet dead serious, predictions of the future was titled "The Face of Tomorrow." It was published in

Public Utilities Fortnightly. One section focused on the home of 1980, thirteen years ahead. It foresaw myriad innovations in the home—most of which were acknowledged to be expensive but would be paid for by an increasingly affluent society.

Dusting is a burdensome chore. By 1980 it would be unnecessary. A built-in device would continually circulate the air, sucking the dust from it. That innovation would also function selectively to remove odors from household air and to add others. Like the smell of lilacs? With this device you could add that smell while at the same time removing the unpleasant smell of bacon frying.

Noisy appliances, like vacuum cleaners, would also be eliminated through better engineering. No matter that consumers connect loud vacuum cleaners and loud lawnmowers with better performance. Engineering rules the roost in these predictions.

Home lighting would also advance. By 1980 entire walls would glow, with less glare than current light bulbs or fluorescent tubes. According to the author, it "costs a little more and it takes more electricity, but this is something we are going to have in the eighties."[3] He offered no reason why. With two strikes—higher purchase costs and higher operating expenses—against it, this innovation was at a severe disadvantage.

Garbage disposals would also become more versatile. By 1980 they would accept paper, which by then could not be thrown away. The disposal would shred the paper and feed it into the sewer system. Clearly, municipalities on the receiving end of this wonder were not enchanted.

Finally, there is the chore of bed-making. According to this forecaster, "Women have to make the beds every day, day after day." By 1980 a machine would do it for her. "I cannot tell you about it until the Patent Office has acted, but I can assure you we are going to have a bed making machine" (p. 38). The bed-making machine never appeared. Furthermore, statements that attribute mundane household chores exclusively to women disappeared by 1980.

In August of 1967 *Fortune* tried its hand at predicting the home of the future. In an article by Lawrence Mayer titled "Home Goods: But What Will They Think of Next" the magazine looked at the prospects for household goods in the next five years.

Home goods would benefit from favorable demographics. Household formations would increase as the baby boom aged, creating a need for home goods. The writer was right, but he failed to foresee the specific home goods that consumers would clamor for.

The fact that consumers owned more than one radio, almost one in every room of the house, caused some forecasters to see a similar trend for other home goods. They predicted there would be a washer-dryer in every bedroom. One executive argued that it "makes sense for all homes to contain at least two units of every small appliance."[4] It never happened. There is no need to waste space and money on such devices.

Some forecasters foresaw "small cooking units in recreation rooms or on terraces" (p. 115). It is difficult to fathom exactly what they had in mind with this prediction, but gas barbecues placed on decks went on to become a consumer favorite in subsequent years. Whether those classify as small cooking units is difficult to ascertain.

The home goods industry regularly needs blockbuster products to maintain growth. Color TV, a recent blockbuster, was believed to be fading—"its most rapid gains almost certainly lie behind it" (p. 117). It was not. Color TV sales grew steadily for many years after.

There was no clear blockbuster on the horizon, but there were possible breakthroughs. The home dry cleaner was one. The microwave oven was another possibility. So was the ultrasonic dishwashing machine, which used sound waves to beat the dirt off dishes. The ultrasonic clothes washer could also turn into a hit by the mid-1970s. Ultrasonics was believed capable of many wonders in the 1960s.

Who says the Fortune 500 are not innovative? In May 1971 *Fortune* presented "Some of the 500's new products."[5] According to the magazine each of the products described was developed or marketed for the first time in 1970.

Among the home products described in the article was the "cool top" range. Developed by Westinghouse, this new approach to cooking used an oscillating magnetic circuit to excite molecules in food. The key advantage was that only the food got "excited," and consequently heated. A piece of paper, or a hand, would not be burned on the "cool top" range. A key draw-back was that the range required the use of cast-iron or steel pots, and it cost much more.

To date, the "cool top" range has failed to excite the market place. Microwave ovens roared ahead while GE has been mar-keting a 12-inch portable induction hotplate (coolplate) for $130, on sale.

In the mid-1960s electricity use was expected to grow expo-nentially—largely because of cheap nuclear power. Gadgets ga-lore would grace our lives. Electric heating elements would be placed in driveways to melt snow the instant it hit the ground. Outdoor barbecuing would be possible in the coldest of winters. Curtains of heated air would shield those once-chilly chefs from the elements.

In 1959 *Newsweek* dedicated an entire issue to the coming dec-ade. The magazine took the task seriously: "Newsweek's editors and the worldwide staff have explored and evaluated tremendous masses of information (millions upon millions of words)." They "talked to hundreds of people." Their goal was "to get the best possible answers to the big questions everyone is asking and will be asking." For example, "What shape will the nation take—where and how will people live, what will they do? . . . What new products will make life better and easier?"[6] Given their rec-ord, maybe they should have looked at billions and billions.

Not surprisingly, the editors and staff were right on some points but mistaken on many others. They correctly foresaw that the coming decade would, economically at least, be aptly called the "Golden Sixties." They also foresaw the replacement of prop planes by jets and predicted the continued shift in population to the Western United States, two clear hits obtained by extrapolat-ing earlier trends.

They foresaw continued rapid growth for the electronics in-dustry, the world's fastest-growing business at the time. As an executive for RCA noted in an article titled "The Magic Future": "In years to come it will bring us even greater wonders" (p. 90). He was right. Electronics has continued to grow rapidly.

They failed to foresee fully a major trend in electronics—the domination of the business by Japanese producers, along with the decline of the American producers. But the magazine warned of increased business competition from Russia, Western Europe, and Japan (in that order), noting that Japan had already made considerable inroads into cotton goods at the expense of American business. There is no mention of electronics; only competition in general. It was well known that Japan made junky electronic goods.

Communication would also grow rapidly. The 1960s would be the decade of the microwave transmission—replacing telephone circuits and transoceanic cables. Furthermore, the 1960s would see tremendous growth in solid-state electronics. Those predictions proved largely correct.

They were less successful when they noted that the Post Office was experimenting with facsimile transmission (years ahead of Federal Express's failed ZapMail).

Lastly, Maurice Stans, Director of the U.S. Bureau of the Budget, warned: "The government has to stop living on credit cards." He predicted that the federal budget would grow from "$80 billion projected for fiscal 1961 to a frightening $100 billion in a few years" (p. 40). He was talking about the budget, mind you, not the budget deficit. But, he was clearly on the right track.

Newsweek's forecasts on home life in the 1960s turned in a far worse performance. They describe home life of the 1960s as follows:

> Waking to cool 1970-style music from a tiny phonograph built into her pillow, the housewife yawned, flicked a bedside switch to turn on the electronic recipe-maker, then rose and stepped into her ultrasonic shower. While sound waves cleaned and vigorously massaged her [p. 88].

This scenario tallies three clear misses: the electronic recipe-maker, the ultrasonic shower, and the pillow phonograph—although the mini-phonograph sounds a lot like the Walkman that would appear fifteen years later. But, as is often the case, it was predicted in a different form with a different use.

Other home forecasts were even more appalling. Cooking would be controlled by punch cards. *Newsweek* also foresaw the ubiquitous dust-sucking air system. The videophone would be used for home grocery shopping. Even suburban lawnmowing would be automated. A robot mower would scan the grasstops hourly with its electronic eye and mow in a preprogrammed pattern when the grass signaled a height too high.

As the magazine noted, "all of these push-botton devices, and hundreds of other futuristic gadgets, are far past the dream state. Prototypes for some already exist; others are now being developed. And there are businessmen who are firmly convinced that all are close to being commercially feasible" (p. 88).

By the 1960s the home itself would be very different. It would have plastic floors. Single wall panels—already under development at Westinghouse Electric—would not only heat and cool the interior of the house but illuminate it as well. Those modern walls would change color and tone at the flick of a button to suit the householder's mood.

Autos would also change. They would be smaller, lighter, and lower, and would use more glass and less chrome—not bad, in hindsight. But, according to this study, they would also have gas-turbine engines, and a single stick would control steering, braking, accelerating, and transmission. (Apparently, learning that complex task would be no problem. After all, jet fighter pilots used a similar mechanism.) Oh, yes, there would also be automated highways with preset routing.

There would be new home appliances as well: closed-circuit television to monitor the nursery and electronic (microwave) cookers that would cook a 15-pound turkey in forty-five minutes. One miss and one hit.

Food would change. There would be further growth of frozen foods—a clear hit. But, mistakenly, they predicted there would be synthetic foods with flavors not found in nature.

Newsweek also foresaw "a lifetime, non-exchangeable credit card issued at birth and designed to be inserted into automatic dispensers of packaged goods" (p. 90). To date, the efficiency of this advance has been outweighed by the invasion of privacy it portends. Americans seem willing to put up with inefficiencies to protect their basic civil liberties.

Education would also be automated. "Why should the classroom be less automated than the kitchen?" the noted Harvard psychologist B. F. Skinner asked (p. 114). There would be educational programs bounced off high-flying planes into schools.

TV correspondence courses would grow as lessons were beamed directly into homes. Some schools would offer "a complete audio-visual experience" (p. 116). And—you guessed it—programmed learning would free teacher's time and allow students to progress at their own pace.

The media would change too. We were entering the great age of home entertainment—a difficult one to evaluate, but a possible hit. There would be wall-size TV screens, international TV, and widespread color TV. Pay TV would grow, but its form was unclear—pay-per-view was being tested. Finally, videotape machines would be built into TV sets for time shifting. (The first Sony Betamax was built into a Trinitron. Only after consumers realized that they already had a TV set did the manufacturer unbundle the system.)

In the political arena, *Newsweek* asks, "Who will be the next president?" The experts picked Nixon in 1960. They foresaw no world war, but many small wars—China might attack Formosa (Taiwan), Arabs and Israelis would fight, and Iraq would war with the United Arab Republic.

Newsweek echoed a familiar refrain: "Events are sure to move more swiftly, not less so, in the ten years to come" (p. 34). It seems that things were moving ever faster in the 1960s, as well as today.

Finally, leisure time would expand greatly, and Americans would have a tough time trying to figure out what to do with themselves. One solution was travel to exotic places. The magazine predicted that by 1970 "Safaris in Vietnam" would be a popular attraction "for the tourist who really wants to get away from it all" (p. 54). Ironically, that turned out to be an accurate prediction, but in a far different form than intended.

What lessons have been learned from those horrendous errors? Apparently very few. True to form, a 1986 end-of-year *Newsweek* forecast called for the smart home. It too foresees fantastic inventions, although the inventions it sees are more in tune with the so-called microelectronics revolution of the mid-1980s than with the issues of the 1960s.

The magazine reported on a meeting of corporate giants sponsored by the Electronics Industries Association. It boldly described the goal of the conference as "turning the house itself into a servant, capable of everything from starting dinner to keeping an eye on a sick child."[7] Electronics will change our lives greatly, it was argued.

We are moving inexorably toward the intelligent home, it claimed, where household items can be placed under computer control. Microwave ovens, for example, will cook food and send a beep to the bedroom when finished. The system will also allow you to call your house and check the temperature in the basement, or to preheat the hot tub for your arrival. You will have to prove your identity, however; hackers could be a problem, the magazine warned.

The system is a technological wonder. Bedroom video screens display the home's floor plan showing opened doors and windows, and detecting movement. The computer identifies problems, such as with the pool heater, and calls repairmen.

There is but a single drawback to the system. It currently cost $500,000. As the Editor of *Electronic House*, a hobbyists' magazine, notes: "You have to keep it in perspective. For what some of our readers spend, you could hire a servant" (p. 59). It sounds like good advice to me.

The lesson to be learned here is that although we read so much today about how things will change rapidly, the home of the future will probably look pretty much like the home of today—although it will be more convenient and more expensive. Twenty years from now it is likely that homes will be made out of the same materials they are now. Revolutions are unlikely. Appliances will perform a wider variety of functions more efficiently, but generally we will still store food in refrigerators, cook most foods before eating them, and be required to exert some effort to accomplish household tasks. What will change will be based on economics, not a love of technological wonder. One GE executive noted recently, "The consumer is only going to respond to something that gives him real benefits easily and at a lower cost" (p. 59). Now, *there* is a worthwhile prediction!

Not all predictions about the home of the future performed badly. A few came close to providing a picture of home products available today. One of the best was *Fortune*'s January 1967 examination of "Where the Industries of the Seventies Will Come From." It foresaw grand visions of computers and entertainment devices in the home. It reported that GE and other firms were envisioning commonplace home computers. Those computers would be tied into a large centralized computer utility. The computer would be used for home banking, calculating taxes, school homework, and storing recipes. Family members would be able to make theater and plane reservations, engage in home shopping, and read books and newspapers on the screen. They would be able to obtain current stock prices and other financial information. The magazine stated: "There now seems no doubt that the computer will have as great and imponderable an impact as electric current on the generation of new businesses and the regeneration of old ones."[8]

Computers would become a key component of the home's entertainment center. That center would include TV, FM radio, and video recorders. A facsimile machine might also be included. Home computer printers would be commonplace.

Those forecasts overstated the potential for many home information services and missed the move away from mainframes to personal computers. The merits of many information services, such as home banking, remain unproved. Furthermore, balancing checkbooks and storing recipes is still, as many believed then, a ridiculous reason to purchase a home computer. Paper does the job much better. Reading books and newspapers on the screen has few advantages over paper versions. It is also more difficult to put them under your arm and bring them with you. Airline reservations are computerized, but not in the home. But financial data retrieval services and library abstracts have proved to be commercially viable markets. Furthermore, video recorders, and now facsimile machines, have spawned huge growth markets. Overall, this vision of the future home turned out to be more accurate than others made at the time. Unfortunately, such visions are also far rarer.

4

A Bias Toward Optimism

As you have undoubtedly surmised, most technological forecasts are far too optimistic. Optimism results from being enamored of technological wonder. It follows from focusing too intently on the underlying technology. The technology suggests wonder, the market usually accepts less.

Only a few technological innovations have warranted the extreme optimism held for them. Only a few innovations have changed our everyday lives as greatly as the forecasters believed they would. VCRs and microwave ovens, for example, and in a more general sense, computers and information, have lived up to the high hopes forecasters had for them. More typically, technological forecasters have seen greater visions than they should have.

Claiming that technological forecasts are overly optimistic is not revolutionary. In 1976 Avison and Nettler, writing in *Futures*, found a strong, and unwarranted, tendency toward overoptimism in the forecasts they studied. They concluded that "a conservative and pessimistic attitude tends to illuminate the crystal ball, while a liberal and optimistic attitude tends to darken it."[1] I agree. As the technological forecasts examined in previous chapters so clearly illustrate, outcomes are usually far less radical than those predicted. Only rarely do growth market forecasts warrant the optimism applied to them.

In 1987 Tyzoon Tyebjee conducted some experiments on biases in new product forecasting. The results were reported in a special issue of the *International Journal of Forecasting* on forecasting in marketing.[2] He found that the very act of participating in the new product planning process led to overly optimistic forecasts. Those involved in the process thought they had more control over the environment than they actually did.

In 1964 Nigel Calder edited a book entitled *The World in 1984*.[3] In it, he had experts from many disciplines make forecasts about their areas of expertise. In 1984, twenty years later, he reviewed the accuracy of those technological forecasts in a follow-up titled *1984 and Beyond*. He hints at the same conclusion. He is particularly impressed with the performance of Barbara Wooten, a social scientist who made predictions in the 1964 study. She made "forecasts that seemed damp and depressing at the time." In hindsight, however, they turned out to be remarkably accurate. Why? According to Calder, because she presumed "that the pattern of social life would not be remarkably different: it would still be news if a Duke married a Dustman's daughter, still be startling to find a truck driver at a lawyer's dinner party."[4] In many technological forecasts, conservatism helped avoid big errors.

Furthermore, successful innovations usually take longer than expected to diffuse through a population. Everett Rogers, in the third edition of his seminal book *Diffusion of Innovations*, observed that many technologists anticipate the rapid growth of an emerging innovation. He noted, however: "Unfortunately, this is seldom the case. Most innovations, in fact, diffuse at a surprisingly slow rate."[5] Forecasters, it seems, are prone to see big changes when none are in store, and rapid changes when slower changes are more likely.

These observations point up a common difference between successful and failed forecasts. The successes tend to be conservative in their outlook, while the failures foresee fantastic changes. The successes call for smaller, slower changes and reject radical innovations.

Clearly, successful forecasts show a better sense of perspective. But, as Calder notes insightfully in his 1984 follow-up, "common sense is often smothered by special enthusiasm, selective inattention, political prejudice, wishful thinking, or doomsaying" (p. 51). Contrast the following forecasts, some of which called for radical changes, with others that called for more modest changes. Consider the sense of perspective shown by each forecaster.

In 1959 the *New York Times* asked three American historians to offer their predictions of the United States in 1970, a decade ahead. Two of the experts foresaw a future world that would be much different from the one they currently lived in. Those same two experts proved most mistaken.

The first expert overestimated the population of the United States.

The second forecaster foresaw two major trends: (1) "the immense increase in world population, in which the United States will share," and (2) "vast growth of atomic power for purposes of both war and peace."[6] Atomic energy would be used to desalinate sea water. Also, the United States and Russia would lose their dominant positions in the world to China, India, Japan, the Arab world, middle Africa, South America, and middle Europe. As a result, tensions in the world would be reduced and the United States would share its military responsibilities with those new powers. Taxpayers would benefit. No longer would they have to carry the burden of heavy defense budgets.

The third historian, Crane Brinton, proved more accurate. His strategy was different from that of the other two historians. Mostly, he avoided forecasts that called for big changes and predicted more of the same. In his own words:

> I should expect life in these United States then to be substantially what it is now. I suppose that this opinion will not be shared by most of my colleagues, but to me, at least, it is a view dictated by the course of history [p. 77].

Using this frame of reference, he predicted that autos would not be very different from those we had then, but they would crowd roads that were still not adequate. The rivalry between the United States and the Soviet Union would persist. He predicted the average life expectancy for Americans would not increase dramatically. Crime would still be commonplace. There would still be a business cycle, but our position in it by 1970 was anybody's guess. "[I]n spite of economic theorists," there will still be "plenty of gift shoppes, independent grocers, and small gadget makers" (p. 77). Big business and government regulation would not destroy those small businesses. There would probably even be small farmers around, he predicted.

Brinton looked even farther ahead, with equally successful results. He speculated, in 1959, that a similar set of forecasts elicited in 1970 to predict 1980 would read pretty much the same as the forecasts made in 1959. He was right. His forecasting strategy yielded forecasts that were far more accurate than either of his colleagues'.

The *Wall Street Journal* also erred on the side of optimism in the forecasts it offered in its 1966 "Shape of the Future" article titled "Population Rise to Pose Problems, But Efforts Made to Ease Impacts."[7]

Consider the setting of the day. There was a worldwide population explosion, and it was unclear whether the postwar baby boom in the United States had ended. Those were important concerns of the mid-1960s.

The journal predicted that population growth would lead to tremendous economic growth. Most important, growth of 20–44-year-olds would lead to new household formations, which would lead to the need for new homes, new autos, new appliances, and consumables of all sorts. It was clear in the mid-1960s that consumers in those age groups were historically "heavy" purchasers of these types of products.

The National Planning Association (NPA) forecast GNP for a government agency. In 1965 GNP was $629 billion (in 1960 dollars). By 1970 it was expected to reach $748 billion, then soar to $1.1 trillion by 1980. By 1990 it would reach $1.6 trillion. In the year 2000, it would stand at $2.3 trillion.

NPA forecasts assumed that GNP would grow at four times the population rate. Productivity gains would also help.

When interviewed ten years later for an article titled "U.S. Unlikely to Be as Big—or as Rich—as Analysts Thought," an economist at the NPA stated: "There's not much interest in long-range forecasts around here any more, we've been wrong too often."[8] *Both* population forecasts and the GNP forecasts turned out to be grossly optimistic. The direction of the forecasts was right, but their magnitude was not.

Interestingly, a key assumption of the 1966 economic forecasts—that many 20–44-year-olds would lead to robust economic growth—proved correct. Whether by coincidence or by design, as the baby boomers approached the maximum consuming years in the 1980s, the economy boomed to a postwar record. In this case, at least, the timing may have been off, but the structure of the forecasts was correct.

Population growth also meant that educational methods would change radically. It was widely believed that people would be educated in new and different ways. Technology would play a large role in educating our children.

In a 1976 article on education, one expert concluded: "I shudder at how cloudy was that crystal ball." That nicely sums up the accuracy of education forecasts. Even forecasts that called for more flexible content and structure of education proved wrong in the more conservative 1980s, when the emphasis is on a back-to-basics approach to education. The educational experiments of the 1960s died with the decade. They were not indicative of educational trends in the decades ahead.

Still, given the record of the 1966 forecasts, experts queried by the journal looked ahead again in 1976. They foresaw "traveling faculty and educational television to teach adults who can't attend classes on campus." One expert even predicted: "By 2000, it won't be necessary to go to high school every day . . . the whole community will be the classroom."[9] The wonder of it all. In New York City many wayward youths seemed to be educating themselves by this method, to the dismay of city officials.

Over the years, energy forecasts have been wildly optimistic and wildly pessimistic. In retrospect, they have also proved to be wildly inaccurate.

In a 1966 article titled "Huge Nuclear Facilities Will Help the U.S. Meet Surging Power Demand," energy forecasts pointed in one direction—straight up. On top of population and economic growth, energy use would grow mostly from increased per capita consumption. We would be using three times as much energy in the year 2000.[10]

According to the journal, electricity use would grow fastest. The Edison Electric Institute predicted that by the year 2000 nearly every home would be heated by electricity. Granted, they had a vested interest, but it was clear at the time that oil heat was certain to be hurt badly.

Forecasts of supply and cost were equally optimistic. According to the journal, "Despite the surge in demand for energy, the supply is expected to be ample in the years ahead. Moreover, it will cost less than it does today because the means of producing it will become more efficient" (p. 1).

But even with those gains in efficiency, fossil fuels might even be too expensive. Coming on stream was nuclear power, which would be so cheap that it would provide seemingly limitless supplies of energy. No wonder that some large cars got less than 10 mpg in the late 1960s. It was not negligence. It was in tune with the beliefs of the day. There was no need for fuel-efficient cars.

The energy outlook changed dramatically between 1966 and 1976. The forecasts turned as pessimistic in 1976 as they had been optimistic in 1966. Energy was no longer abundant and would cost far more than it had. Nuclear power was on the skids. In 1976 we were not self-sufficient in energy, and we were at the mercy of hostile foreigners. It was unimaginable that by the mid-1980s gas prices would have risen far more slowly than predicted.

Individual, visionary forecasters, even those in places of power and prominence, have fared no better at predicting long-term trends. In 1956, David Sarnoff, the former chairman of RCA, presented a paper entitled "Twenty Years from Now: A Forecast." In it, he described twenty major developments likely to affect us all by 1976. *Forbes* reviewed fourteen of his forecasts more than twenty years after they were made. Its conclusion was that Sarnoff was enamored of technological wonder.

Sarnoff predicted that nuclear energy would be widely used to power industry, ships, trains, and autos. Mail would be delivered by guided missile. There would be a "crescendo" of automation through cheap and abundant power. There would be a generally well-fed world, with accurate year-ahead weather reports. One problem he foresaw was that there would be relative worldwide economic abundance of such magnificence that leisure time would be the most pressing problem (in hindsight, a real problem for the unemployed of the early 1980s).

Lighting would change. Electroluminescent (cool) light would be used to light factories, streets, stores, highways, and homes. Soviet communism would fall. Finally, the SST and the picture telephone would be widely available.

He did get some forecasts right. He predicted that every form of art and entertainment would be readily accessible in the home—a possibility, given the widespread diffusion of videocassette recorders and other home electronic products. He also predicted that computers would be widely used in business—probably as far-fetched a prediction in the precomputer mid-1950s as mail delivered by guided missile. Finally, he predicted that there would be global television and commonplace color television.

Overall, Sarnoff's accuracy rating is roughly 25 percent—a less than enviable record, but better than many of his contemporaries.

Forbes concludes: "Sarnoff's expansive optimism was wide of the mark." It also observes that Sarnoff performed best when he stuck to the areas he knew best. *Forbes* advises, "When you get the urge to predict the future, better lie down until the feeling goes away."[11]

Sarnoff was no stranger to forecasting. *Smithsonian* quotes the then president of RCA as saying in 1939 that "television drama of high caliber and produced by first-rate artists, will materially raise the level of dramatic taste of the nation, just as aural broadcasting has raised the level of music appreciation."[12] His prediction turned out to be overly optimistic. Although many attempts have been made to entice the ordinary citizen to embrace the fine arts, most of the populace seems to prefer the popular entertainment that pervades most of television today.

Furthermore, it is debatable whether music appreciation has increased greatly. Surely the parents of teenagers whose offspring are fond of heavy metal music would disagree. A survey of radio stations would also disagree. Popular music, especially rock-and-roll, makes up much of the offering these days.

Studies by industry groups have turned in similar performances. A late 1960s study by the Insurance Information Institute entitled "A Report on Tomorrow," published by *National Underwriter*, "projects what life will be like in the 1980s." It too foresaw automated highways, orbiting factories in space, undersea hotels, and ready-made houses delivered by helicopter. As the article on the study notes, the report "takes a tone of cautious optimism."[13] Apparently, not cautious enough.

Interestingly, the study performed well on the only forecast that had to do directly with the insurance industry. It predicted that by the 1980s insurance agents would be hawking a wide variety of financial services, blurring the differences between insurance and other providers of financial services. Possibly, expertise is helpful in forecasting, but only when applied to the specific area where the expert is in fact an expert. Expertise may not be generalizable to other areas.

The Value of Discounting Trend Projections

Projecting past trends is one of the most widely used methods of generating growth market forecasts. There are myriad methods to choose from, each with its own set of assumptions and calculations. Some models simply apply straight-line extrapolations to a few years of initial sales figures. Other models, more typical of those found in growth market forecasting, are more aggressive, and hence more prone to severe overoptimism. They postulate that sales will start off slowly, then climb rapidly as the product catches consumer interest. These models assume an accelerating trend.

Trend projections span the spectrum from elaborate mathematical treatments to simple intuitive rules of thumb—next year's sales will be 5 percent higher than this year's sales. The research results are clear on which kinds of extrapolations are best. There is absolutely no evidence that complicated mathematical models provide more accurate forecasts than much simpler models that incorporate intuitively pleasing rules of thumb. In growth market forecasting it seems less important whether the model is fancy or not than whether the model incorporates the right assumptions. A forecast that assumes accelerating growth for a product that goes nowhere is doomed from the start, no matter what level of sophistication is used to implement the assumption. Assuming rapid growth in sales of the picture telephone, for example, would have proved grossly optimistic even had the largest Cray computer been used to generate the forecast. Whatever the level of sophistication, inappropriate assumptions would have resulted in "garbage in, garbage out."

Surprisingly, growth market forecasting methods continue to rely almost exclusively on extrapolations that favor aggressive and optimistic forecasts. Little effort has been expended on moderating trends, although doing so would have lessened the errors of the past. Again, in growth market forecasting we have failed to learn from past mistakes. We go on to repeat them again in the future.

One recent exception is the work of Everette Gardner and Ed McKenzie. In a 1985 article in *Management Science,* they proposed a simple mathematical model that incorporates a "damped" trend.[14] Rather than fitting a straight-line projection or (worse yet) a projection that accelerates the trend, their model bends the trend toward the horizontal if there is historical evidence that growth is slowing. In essence, their model errs on the side of conservatism and avoids highly optimistic forecasts.

They and others, including myself, have tested their model in many different types of applications.[15] Almost universally, it has been found to be more accurate. I strongly suspect it is not the mathematics that matter but the concept of damping the trend. Conservatism pays off in growth market forecasting. Optimism does not. In fact, some of the same studies that have shown an advantage for damping the trend have shown a severe disadvantage for accelerating the trend.

The message is clear. Be conservative in your estimates of the potential for new products based on innovative technologies. "Cut" or damp any trend estimates with which you are provided. Do not be swayed by the sophistication of the forecasting method or the forecaster. Be suspicious. Be especially suspicious of forecasts that are based on accelerating trends in growth. In the past they have led to the largest errors.

The Dangers of Accelerating Trends

It is never advisable to use the word always. One exception exists when it comes to the use of projections based on accelerating trends for technological forecasts. Many technological forecasts have failed because they have projected accelerating growth from only the skimpiest of data. They assumed, incorrectly, that a few periods of early growth were a signal of even stronger growth later on. Most often, such assumptions are unwarranted.

Consider the case of videotex. Videotex is a computer-based

service that allows consumers to shop and bank electronically, as well as access information from their homes and offices. It was expected to serve a mass market but has served only a small niche instead.

The initial videotex product contained text and graphics. In 1983 a market research firm specializing in videotex projected exponential growth. Although only five thousand terminals had been installed, the firm estimated that there would be 1.9 million users by 1988. One year later they revised their forecast downward—to 95,000 users, only 5 percent of the original estimate![16]

Did they learn from their earlier mistake? Apparently not. They then predicted that text-only systems would show exponential growth, rising from less than 500,000 users to 4.2 million users by 1988. Growth turned out to be far more modest.

Many corporate heavyweights pursued the new videotex technology: IBM, Sears, and CBS joined forces in February 1984 to form Trintex; Chemical Bank, Bank of America, Time, and AT&T combined efforts in a unit called Covidea; and Citicorp, RCA, and NYNEX banded together to enter this emerging market. They joined Knight-Ridder Newspapers, the pioneer, and the Times-Mirror Company.

Subsequent market penetration stayed meager. In March 1986 Knight-Ridder and Times-Mirror quit the business after losing $80 million. IBM's commitment remains uncertain. The initial and revised predictions again turned out to have been far too optimistic. The problem, according to an executive at the very firm that issued the forecasts: "There were few if any services that people just felt they had to have."[17] Clearly, common sense had been overruled by optimism in videotex forecasts.

Forecasters are prone to mirages. Their burning thirst for trends leads them to see patterns when there are none. As a result they often see opportunities for spectacular growth without thinking the problem through. In regard to videotex systems, Andrew Pollack, writing in the the *New York Times*, notes: "People still prefer touching the merchandise in a department store to ordering by computer, and reading a newspaper to scanning a video display tube with their morning coffee."[18] He is using common sense.

One of the most stunning examples of a growth market that fizzled was CB radios. That innovation gained consumers' attention when the 55-mph speed limit was imposed in response to the oil embargo of the early 1970s, and the long-haul trucker was venerated for his attempts to evade it. In 1975, sales of CB radios rocketed to $400 million, three times the total of the previous year. Forecasts uniformly called for continued rapid growth, with annual sales reaching $1 billion in 1977. But that was only the beginning; "both the industry and Wall Street say that this hardly scratches the surface of long-range potential. Over the next decade they foresee a market for 75 million to 125 million CB radios."[19]

Major manufacturers, such as General Electric, Motorola, and Texas Instruments, eagerly entered this emerging market. They sought to displace the smaller manufacturers and Japanese imports that pioneered it. The market fizzled shortly after they entered. Beginning in 1977, sales drifted inexorably downward. The primary reason for the turnaround was that consumers simply lost interest in the product and proceeded to the next craze.

Originally, the facsimile machine, or sending mail by phone, was targeted toward business customers. Although a bright future was predicted for those devices, it took nearly twenty years for the product to exhibit rapid growth. Twenty years ago, in 1968, Xerox and Magnavox were joined by Litton, Stewart-Warner, and a host of other entrants in an attempt to garner the lion's share of this growth market. They all believed it was "on the verge of a boom akin to that of the office copier."[20] One executive predicted that sales would climb to 500,000 units in just a few years, even though only 4,000 were currently in use for business correspondence.

The innovation failed to catch fire. It was too expensive and took too long to send a single document—ten 8 1/2-by-11-inch sheets in an entire day! No wonder companies called the courier.

By 1987 the situation had changed. Prices had been reduced dramatically, and performance had increased. Driven by consumer and small business purchases, sales skyrocketed to nearly 300,000 units in 1987. After twenty years, the balance between price and performance finally stirred a growth market for this innovation and warranted the optimism that had originally been applied to it. In the case of facsimile machines, change came much more slowly than expected.

Bias in Diffusion of Innovation Research

Much of the work that has been done in growth market forecasting has its roots in an academic discipline called the diffusion of innovation. The discipline cuts across areas of study as diverse as rural sociology (where it has successfully persuaded farmers, traditionally a very noninnovative group, to accept and use new types of crops), marketing, anthropology, communications, and economics.

The diffusion of innovation is concerned with the flow of new products from their invention to their widespread use. Beginning in the 1960s, marketing embraced the diffusion of innovation tradition. With varying degrees of success, marketers looked at cases where experts were able to get primitive villagers in Third World countries to boil water so they would not get sick. They then tried to apply the principles of those cases to modern markets.

A central thesis of diffusion of innovation is that some initial group of customers purchase new products. They are called the innovators. In primitive societies innovators tend to be oddballs, or eccentrics, who are not strongly tied to the culture and the current way of doing things. After a while, a second group of customers, opinion leaders, enters the market. Rapid market growth ensues as many other consumers imitate the purchases of these respected members of society. Sales soar until the market saturates. Then growth slows, as nearly everyone is using the product. In a nutshell, diffusion of the product is hypothesized to follow an S-shaped curve—slow sales followed by rapid growth, followed by slow sales.

Consider the diffusion of black-and-white TVs in the United States, a frequently used example. Initially, only a few households adopted the product. Then, in the mid-1950s, sales skyrocketed. When just about everyone owned at least one black-and-white TV, the market was saturated. Currently, over 90 percent of the households in the United States own a black-and-white TV.

Related concepts, such as the product life cycle (PLC), propose similar patterns, although they approach the problem from a different perspective. The PLC holds that when a new product is placed on the market, initial sales are slow. But slow sales are replaced by rapid sales growth as the product gains consumer interest. Marketers call this the growth stage of the PLC. Ultimately, growth slows as the market saturates. Decline then sets in as another innovation takes over. In its purest form, the PLC holds that sales follow an S-shaped pattern, until they decline.

Finally, numerous studies have postulated growth curves for new technological products. Those curves follow a similar pattern to the previous formulations. In fact, many growth curves have their theoretical roots in either the diffusion of innovation or PLC tradition. The curves invariably project strong growth.

Typically, forecasts based on these formulations use a few initial estimates of growth and project them into the future. Another popular scheme is to use judgments made by experts or managers, which are then plugged into mathematical models that project trends.

The problem with using research arising out of the diffusion of innovations, the product life cycle, and market growth curves is that they ignore the fact that market growth is not guaranteed, or even likely. Forecasts based on those theories have a built-in tendency to be overly optimistic. They all presuppose strong market growth. They say nothing of failure. Consequently, they set up firms to repeat the same errors. By their very nature these research traditions, when applied to growth market forecasting, result in overly optimistic projections of market growth.

There is no law, nor even an inherent tendency, for products to exhibit the growth implied by these formulations. In fact, most new products fail. Nearly every study that has looked at the issue has concluded that most new products never make it. They never progress through any of these patterns. They never make it out of stage one.

This is not to suggest that the work in these areas is flawed. It is not. It is simply not very useful for growth market forecasting. Most of the work in these areas is concerned with describing how innovations that have already been successful have diffused through the population. Since, by definition, the work is concerned only with products that have already exhibited strong market growth, these models project strong market growth. But, since the theories rely so heavily on after-the-fact explanations, they are of little help in predicting which technologies will go on to spawn huge growth markets and which will repeat previous failures.

You will never see the PLC applied to 3-D TV, the picture telephone, or other failed innovations. It is applied only to successful innovations, such as black-and-white or color TV, which have already demonstrated substantial growth. It also offers no mechanism for distinguishing between products that will grow to dizzying heights and products that will go nowhere.

Most important, initial sales offer little indication of subsequent growth. Any curve, or set of curves, can only serve to mislead. Future sales will be determined by fundamental marketing factors. It is a mistake to assume that trends and patterns have a life of their own. They do not. Theories and models that assume that they do will mislead you and result in overly optimistic forecasts.

5

The Zeitgeist

In 1937 Sir Frank Whittle, a British inventor, successfully tested the first jet aircraft engine. By coincidence, Hans von Ohain, a competing German scientist, produced a similar engine that same year. When asked how two scientists—unknown to each other and unaware of each other's work—could develop the same device, Sir Frank replied: "The tree of scientific knowledge tends to bear its fruit at the same time."[1] As this chapter will illustrate, forecasts seem to grow in the same orchard.

Technological forecasts made at the same time tend to foresee the same events. Forecasts made in the 1960s, for example, consistently envisioned extensive space travel, automated roadways, and the use of jet and nuclear technology in myriad applications. Today we would never make the same predictions. Forecasts made during the 1970s focused on energy devices that would help solve the then current crises. Today we seem to have forgotten about those issues. Clearly, each era has its own important issues.

Unfortunately, the issues of one period have little to do with the issues of another. They are descriptive of the present rather than the future. As a result, technological forecasts tell more about the times in which they were made than they do about the times they seek to predict. Forecasters are inextricably bound up in the spirit of the times in which they live. It is an inescapable condition of long-term forecasting, which greatly colors forecasts made at any one time period.

It is remarkably easy to ascertain the decade in which a technological forecast was made. Although past forecasts are often unable to predict the times ahead, they indicate the spirit of the times when they were made.

Popular beliefs about the implications of a new technology also change over time, even though at any one time they show an amazing consensus. Consider the movie *Metropolis*, made in an earlier part of this century. It mirrored the widespread belief of the day that industrial automation would enslave workers rather than free them from drudgery. By the 1960s the perception had changed: Automation would result in increased leisure time for a carefree populace.

How does that occur? Why do forecasters tend to foresee the same events simultaneously? Why are forecasts more indicative of the times in which they are made than of the times they seek to predict? How could such a consensus be achieved on predictions that, in retrospect, turned out to be horrendous errors?

One hypothesis is that forecasters simply copy each other's forecasts and repeat the same mistakes. It is more likely that forecasters deduce similar conclusions after an examination of the same body of information available to all forecasters at the time.

The Zeitgeist concept is used to explain the fact that inventions and discoveries tend to be made simultaneously by researchers working independently. Like the example of the jet engine described above, Watson's and Crick's discovery of the DNA double helix beat competing efforts by only a short time. Had Watson and Crick pursued careers in professional sports, say, rather than science, the double helix would have been discovered at roughly the same time by another team. It would not have remained undiscovered for long.

Zeitgeist implies that many discoveries are made in this fashion: Present conditions hold the seeds for future technological developments, and those seeds can germinate in many minds at once. Consequently, the Zeitgeist means that inventions and discoveries are due less to the power of individual genius than to the spirit of the times.

As the review of previous forecasts suggests, technological forecasters are influenced similarly. Each has the same general information to study, as well as a common historical perspective. As a result, similar times breed similar forecasts and, as a result, similar errors.

The concept of the Zeitgeist holds that there is a characteristic spirit of the times marked by a predominant feature that characterizes the intellectual, political, and social trends of that era. By implication, the Zeitgeist idea holds that forecasters are imprisoned by the spirit of the times in which they live. This is not to say that forecasters simply make straight-line projections, although the practice is certainly common, but that they are anchored to the present by the issues of their day and frame their forecasts in terms of those issues. Many of the forecasts proffered during the 1960s were unduly influenced by the unprecedented economic growth of the decade and the prominence of the space race. In the 1970s energy issues were preeminent.

The Zeitgeist also casts doubts on the merits of consensus forecasts. It implies that a consensus forecast is not difficult to obtain, but that the consensus may be more indicative of present beliefs than of actual future outcomes. TRW's "Probe" of the future was based on a consensus, yet its forecasts failed miserably. The experts agreed, but they agreed on the wrong things. The most insidious influence of the Zeitgeist may be that it fools many rather than a few.

Consider another study based explicitly on consensus. In 1973, DuPont, Scott Paper, Lever Brothers, and Monsanto funded "Project Aware," a comprehensive Delphi study conducted by the prestigious Institute of the Future. The study was "a unique attempt to predict long-range changes in the social, economic, and technological environment that the companies will face in the next decade."[2] The experts who participated in the study reached a consensus that there was a 90 percent probability that National Health Insurance would be enacted by 1985. However, with deficits over $150 billion, lawmakers have been reluctant to advocate yet another expensive program.

Kaiser Aluminum fared no better with a consensus-generating technique. In 1966 they conducted a Delphi study called "Future." The study had experts estimate the probability that each of sixty events would occur within the next twenty years, by 1986. Some of the forecasts were published in a 1967 issue of *The Iron Age*.[3] Most of the forecasts were stated vaguely and hence were difficult to evaluate.

The experts foresaw the greatest likelihood (80 percent) of the following events: Worldwide production of fresh water from

the oceans would be economic; investment in automated equipment would be ten times that in 1966; there would be widespread use of lasers and ultra-light metal substitutes. The article
is silent on the issue that most characterized the future of the
industry: the inexorable decline of domestic steel production. It
was not that the experts got the probabilities wrong, but they
did not consider the right issues. Instead of the issues of the
future, they focused on the issues of their own time.

In 1957 E. F. Hutton & Company, the investment house,
asked twenty-five executives of major firms to predict what industries would be like in 1979, twenty-two years ahead. Hutton
buried the results in a time capsule in its Manhattan office. In
1979 the capsule was opened on the firm's seventy-fifth anniversary. The *Wall Street Journal* evaluated the performance of the
forecasts in 1979. The results were typical. The forecasts were
wildly optimistic. Bad eyesight would be cured by pills. There
would be widespread supersonic travel. Most households would
have 3-D TV. The journal concludes that "there was a markedly
optimistic tone to all the predictions: Americans could do anything if they put their minds to it." Most notably, the reaction to
the forecasts in 1979 was as much influenced by the events of
1979 as the forecasters had been by the spirit of the times in
1957. In reaction to the 1957 forecasts, one broker stated: "It
isn't like today, where you have a feeling of helplessness, that
problems *can't* be solved."[4] That reaction captures the malaise
that Jimmy Carter talked about. The gross optimism of the late
1950s gave way to the pessimism of the 1970s, which in turn
gave way to the renewed optimism of the 1980s.

Most technological forecasts fail not because of mistakes in
fine tuning. They fail big. The Zeitgeist ensures that they will
stress the present rather than the future.

Dominant Themes of the Day

The history of technological forecasting has been heavily colored
by a changing series of "dominant themes of the day." That is,
over the years forecasters have focused on different technological innovations, each of which was expected to have far-reaching
effects on our lives. Those forecasts have typically proved

wrong. Few of the dominant themes carry over into subsequent decades. They dissipate and are replaced by new dominant themes.

Consider some of the failures that have resulted from overemphasizing the dominant technology of the day.

The Jet Engine

In the early 1950s the British introduced the first commercial jet aircraft—the De Haviland. Consumer enthusiasm for the jet stalled with early crashes. The Boeing 707 was introduced in 1958. By the early 1960s jet aircraft were the rage. Many predictions at the time called for emerging markets based on the widespread application of jet technology. Surely, it was believed, an innovation as important as jet engines would be used for more than simply transporting air passengers more quickly to their destinations. Jet technology, it was believed, would diffuse to many other markets.

For example, in 1966 industry experts predicted, "The shipping industry appears ready to enter the jet age."[5] It was a logical extension of the pattern that had been followed in air transport, where jets replaced prop planes. By 1968, large cargo ships powered by gas turbine engines were expected to penetrate the commercial market. The benefits of that innovation were greater reliability, quicker engine starts, and shorter docking times. According to the experts, there was only one real disadvantage: In 1966 the fuel for these ships cost twice that of regular engines. Apparently, that was considered a minor drawback at the time.

The analogy between ships and planes proved mistaken. Jet engines led to efficiencies in airplanes but not in ships. Furthermore, ships could be powered by cheap and heavy fuels, such as coal and diesel fuel.

Cars would also move into the jet age. All three American automakers spent heavily on turbine cars using jet technology. The transfer of technology from airplanes to autos failed to generate a growth market. It was an impractical idea. Possibly, engineers at those firms should have spent their time more wisely. In this case, their concern with technological innovation was misplaced. The true threat lay elsewhere. The industy's lack of concern for imports is captured by a 1961 quote from *Business*

Week: "The U.S. industry's compact cars have slammed the door on the market for imported family sedans costing around $2,000."[6] Apparently, the U.S. manufacturers got their foot caught in the door. While domestic producers pursued jet cars, the Japanese concentrated on making less exotic products better. The result was a boom in imports and a bust in jet cars—and, ironically, a near bust for Chrysler, a key jet car proponent.

Similarly, we hear a great deal today from the automakers about how new technologies will be contained in cars of the future. Fantastic inventions, like in-car radar screens to see wild animals ahead in foggy weather and satellite-aided navigation, are predicted as important innovations in the future. They capture the widespread belief that our lives will be replete with technological wonder. Meanwhile, Hyundai sets sales records with lower prices, albeit without the radar screens.

An early 1988 GM auto display of cars of the future put on for shareholders repeated those same themes of technological wonder. In addition to the radar screens, steering wheels were on the way out. They would be replaced by two "joy sticks" like the kind used to play video games. The public would maneuver a car with a steering mechanism similar to that used in helicopters. This device replaced an earlier vision of future steering, popular in the 1960s, which relied on a single stick like that used to steer early jet fighters.

In defense of domestic producers it must be noted that the Japanese have been criticized for failing to open their markets to American producers. The Japanese assure us that this will soon change. Interestingly, the Japanese have been making the same assurances since at least 1961. In 1961 *Business Week* reported, "The Japanese assure the U.S. and other industrialized nations that they will continue an import liberalization plan."[7]

Apparently their plan is continuing to move forward—at a less than frantic pace. After more than a quarter of a century they are still making the same assurances.

Auto design was greatly influenced by the jet. During the 1950s and into the 1960s, the ubiquitous tail fin symbolized the car of the future. The idea for the tail fin came directly from jet technology. Car tail fins were copied from jet fighters of the late 1940s. Artificial air intakes, similar to those on jets, were also common on cars in the 1950s. In the 1950s, to be like a jet was to be modern.

The ultimate manifestation of the "jet age" was the SST. Until the 1960s there was a clear trend toward faster and faster airplanes. The next logical step in the progression was the SST. Throughout the 1950s many nations contemplated the development of an SST. A popular refrain was: "The technology is there." In 1963 President Kennedy signaled government support for a U.S. program. Costs flew faster than the plane. In 1969 President Nixon appointed a committee to study the project. It found numerous environmental and economic problems. In 1971 Congress killed project funding. Britain and France pursued the project. Their Concordes found buyers only among the captive airlines of their respective countries.

Interestingly, some forecasters in the 1960s were looking even farther ahead. They foresaw the HST—hypersonic transport—which went faster yet. This invention seemed to die with the SST, until President Reagan resurrected it during a speech in 1986.

There is now growing interest among aerospace companies in funding for the hypersonic transport. According to advocates, these planes would reach 17,000 mph, cutting the time of a London-to-Sydney trip to a mere sixty-seven minutes. One Lockheed expert who is bullish on the project proclaims, "We're where we were in 1953 or '54 when we saw that jet transportation was practical."[8] Send aspirin instead of money. It sounds like he has the fever.

The Space Race

Similarly, the space race of the late 1950s and 1960s greatly colored many predictions of the day. The emphasis on space technology caused by President Kennedy's promise to place a man on the moon by the end of the decade was inexorably carried forward into the 1970s and beyond. The moon landing was merely the first step in a progression of events toward the further exploration of space, it was widely believed. Most predictions incorrectly assumed that the moon landing would be followed by space stations, manned trips to Mars, and other elaborate and expensive projects. Given that set of assumptions, forecasters foresaw permanent, manned lunar bases, space stations, commercial passenger rockets, and frequent visits to other planets, all in a setting where children wanted to grow up to be astronauts rather than computer wizards. People were fascinated by space travel. Few recognized that the tremendous growth in the program would be limited to the 1960s. After landing a man on the moon, space was deemphasized. In the 1970s, attention shifted elsewhere.

Some companies were ready to exploit the market that space travel would surely bring. In 1957 the President of Plough Inc., the drug company now named Schering-Plough Corp., predicted that the firm "would be looking for a remedy for physical upsets caused by possible pressure, temperature and other changes incidental to interplanetary travel."[9]

The leadoff article of a 1967 seven-part series on the "Shape of the Future" in the *Wall Street Journal* focused on the future of space exploration. It was entitled "Manned Mars Landing, Moon Base Are Seen as Likely Space Feats." The article reflected the widespread beliefs of the day in regard to where space exploration was headed in the years ahead. Typical of predictions made during that period were the pronouncements of one expert: "By the year 2000 we will undoubtedly have a sizable operation on the moon, we will have achieved a manned Mars landing and it's entirely possible we will have flown with men to the outer planets." Undoubtedly, it turned out we did none of those things. And it seems we are moving farther away from accomplishing them as the century draws to a close.

One of the primary reasons why we have deemphasized extensive manned space travel in the 1980s was present in the late-1960s, but wishful thinking and a preference for following past trends clouded the future outlook. The newspaper noted that "money will be the main obstacle."[10] It surely was. The manned Mars mission alone would cost between $40 billion and $100 billion. The nuclear rocket would be needed. "Space tugs" were also essential. Not to worry. The benefits from those huge expenditures in the space program would be great indeed. We would get more accurate weather forecasts, greater knowledge of our surroundings, and space rocks galore. Besides, we had to do it—the Russians were going, the Russians were going! We could not let them beat us.

Nuclear Energy

Nuclear energy was expected to be a dominant technology of the 1980s. Predictions of the 1950s and 1960s almost universally saw a bright future for nuclear power. Not only would electric utilities adopt the technology, but other sectors of the economy would also switch to this modern energy source.

The *Wall Street Journal* saw a bright future for nuclear energy in a 1966 article entitled "Huge Nuclear Facilities Will Help U.S. Meet Surging Power Demand." Looking forward, it saw that "there will be almost limitless supplies of power from nuclear power plants, expected eventually to be the cheapest source of energy almost everywhere on the globe."

Utilities had their work cut out for them. The forecasts showed that they should build nuclear, and build fast and big. A key concern was whether utilities could build nuclear plants fast enough to meet the expected surge in demand. By the year 2000, it was predicted, all large power plants would be nuclear, and the last of the old oil-fired plants would shut down.

Breeder reactors would be in use by 1985. They represented the next step in a logical flow of developments in nuclear energy.

At the time, many worried that those estimates would prove too conservative. Past predictions of electricity use had been revised sharply upward. The same was likely to occur this time.

Increased electric use would lead to many growth markets as electric products supplanted products based on other forms of power. Westinghouse predicted that all railroads would switch to electric power by the end of the century. Critics suggested that the gas turbine would be the more attractive alternative to diesel locomotion. Whichever alternative won, from the perspective of 1966 it was clear that diesel locomotives were on the way out.

It seemed certain that ships would also go nuclear. According to an official at the Federal Maritime Administration, by the year 2000 nuclear ships "will be counted in the hundreds."[11]

In 1966 there was but a single nuclear merchant ship—the *Savannah*. Much larger nuclear ships would come, it was predicted. Instead the industry declined and few, if any, commercial ships—nuclear or not—were built in U.S. yards. David Klinges, president of marine construction for Bethlehem Steel, noted recently that "we can't build a ship in an American shipyard even if we had no labor costs at all."[12] Again, while we pursued technological wonder, others beat us with basics.

The forecasts also missed the key issues. While we foresaw an industry replete with technological advances, we missed the inexorable decline that followed and were unprepared for it. The forecasts served to seduce, to instill a false sense that the industry would be saved by our ability to stay one step ahead of the competition with new technology. By looking ahead with unrealistic expectations, we fell behind.

Many forecasters believed that nuclear power would be widely used to power autos. That would be possible because nuclear reactors would shrink to very small sizes. Nuclear auto engines would be the size of a man's fist. A 1985 Smithsonian Institution exhibition included the "Nucleon," Ford's 1958 nuclear-powered car. The very fact that it ended up as a museum piece tells much about its fate.

Industrial uses of nuclear power would also be commonplace. Factories would be nuclear-powered. Small reactors might even be placed on tall towers to act as small suns, finally placing the weather under man's control. Nuclear wonders would be everywhere.

Rockets would be nuclear-powered. During the 1950s and 1960s the U.S. Government spent a fortune on research into a nuclear rocket engine that would heat liquid hydrogen, which would push the rocket skyward. Believe it or not, the project was called Rover. In hindsight, it turned out to be a dog and was abandoned in the early 1970s. The program never produced a rocket that lifted off the ground.

Is it now apparent that the program was caught up in the spirit of the times? Apparently not. In 1987 the Air Force resurrected the program. One official noted: "We'll be using the last small engine from the Rover program." The project manager is calling for a national effort in nuclear propulsion. The project is needed to move supplies from orbiting space shuttles to more distant points in space. Most appealing, the project would save money. One Air Force lieutenant in charge of the project noted: "The higher performance of nuclear engines allows us to reduce operational costs, saving the government money."[13] Don't count on it.

In 1961, *Business Week* reported that the nuclear-powered rocket was a major market opening up for robotics.[14] It was clear that the nuclear rocket was on the way. Another technology, robotics, would tag along. Interestingly, robotics, although widely predicted as an emerging trend in the early 1960s, did not accelerate until the mid-1980s.

Some forecasters even foresaw uses for nuclear power in construction projects. In 1965, the chairman of the Atomic Energy Commission testified before a Congressional committee that by 1967 it would be ready to use a nuclear device "to blast a two-mile-long cut through the Bristol Mountains of Southern California."[15] This road and railway project would be followed by the blasting of a "second Panama Canal." The citizenry would be exposed to only "reduced" amounts of radioactivity. No wonder Nicaragua speaks ill of us.

The commission had done its homework. The benefits of the programs—their efficiency—were clearly in line with the costs. Unfortunately, to the dismay of construction technologists, the spirit of the times changed. The perception of nuclear energy in the 1950s and 1960s as a modern, too-inexpensive-to-meter, cutting-edge advancement changed to that of a dangerous, unmanageable technology in the 1980s.

A researcher at the California Institute of Technology had a better idea for constructing roads. He suggested that nuclear reactors be used to "melt" highways directly into the landscape. The heat of the reactor could be used to turn dirt into an artificial lava, which would be smooth enough for a road surface. That process was more efficient than traditional approaches to road-building. It also turned out to be socially and politically unacceptable.

In 1979 Sam Love, writing in the *Smithsonian*, reviewed many of the predictions for nuclear power published in the popular press. First, it was widely believed that nuclear power would be so cheap that it would not pay to meter it. Second, that was expected to lead to veritable miracles in our lives. In 1955, for example, Harold Stassen foresaw cordless lamps, irons, toasters, bedmakers, and motorless appliances of all sorts as a result of nuclear energy. He stated: "Yes, these things are fantastic [yet] with low-cost, limitless power—and that's what atomic energy is potentially—all sorts of dreams can come true."[16] For some, the dream turned into a nightmare.

Interestingly, an early pioneer of electricity, who in 1915 offered the same cost forecast for electricity that others later used for nuclear power, stated that "it will not pay to install meters" (p. 87). He was talking about electricity, not nuclear power.

Oddly, no serious forecasts foresaw the turning point for nuclear energy. Forecasting the demise of nuclear energy in the 1950s and 1960s was akin to forecasting a decline in oil prices in the 1980s during the energy crunch of the 1970s. No one would publish such an outlandish prediction, and, surely, no one would believe it. Such predictions would have been out of sync with the spirit of the times.

The Energy Crisis

Technological wonder gave way to the scarcity mentality of the 1970s. During the 1970s scarcity was a dominant theme of most forecasts. Investors fell over each other in their quest for tangible assets. The spirit of the times held that oil prices would continue to rise, as would farm prices and prices of many other raw materials. From the perspective of the 1970s, we were finally running up against the age of limits to our resources.

Many firms acquired raw material companies. They were pursuing the issues of the 1970s in order to excel in the 1980s. Mostly, they were trapped by their beliefs, reinforced by the experts.

Imagine yourself in the late 1970s forecasting that energy prices would decline throughout the 1980s. For one, it never would have happened. Such a forecast would have been preposterous at the time. All the indicators of the day pointed to ever higher oil prices. Some even talked of the end of the petroleum age. Even if you had made the forecast, who would have believed it? It was inconsistent with the beliefs of the day.

Ultrasonics

Ultrasonics was another "hot" technology, albeit an odd one. In the 1960s many forecasts called for widespread application of ultrasonic technology. *Newsweek* predicted that we would be taking ultrasonic showers by 1970. Water would be obsolete, and dirt would be beaten off your body by sound waves.[17]

In 1967, *Fortune* foresaw "ultrasonic cleaning for dishes—and perhaps even for clothes."[18]

Similarly, the *Wall Street Journal* saw a bright future for the ultrasonic dishwasher in a 1967 article titled: "Electronic Wizardry Will Transform Life in Tomorrow's Homes."[19] In addition, this report foresaw a device that would remove dirt from clothes as homeowners entered their homes.

A few years later *Fortune* again looked forward in an article entitled "Some of the 500s New Products." It described the ultrasonic sewing machine, developed by Branson Sonic Power, a subsidiary of Smith, Kline & French Laboratories. This innovation used high-frequency vibrations to "weld," rather than stitch, synthetic fabrics. Its primary advantage was that it could sew (weld) fast—a buttonhole in less than one second. According to the article, the ultrasonic sewing machine "enables every girl to step out without a stitch."[20]

The ultrasonic sewing machine possessed only a few minor disadvantages. First, it worked only on synthetic fibers—but it was clear, at the time, that synthetics were quickly gaining market share on old-fashioned fabrics like cotton, which could not be welded. Second, ultrasonic "welds" were permanent; once made, they could not be undone. Consequently, shifting hemlines caused a problem for the Branson ultrasonic sewing machine. More important, a shift in social trends toward woman working outside the home and away from home sewing of any type spelled the decline of this market. Singer, the best-known manufacturer of nonultrasonic sewing machines, now concentrates on avionics. In fact, it withdrew from the sewing business in the late 1980s. Ultrasonics turned out to be a doomed technology aimed at a dying market.

In 1960 the *Harvard Business Review* published "Marketing Myopia," one of the most influential articles ever published in the field of Marketing. The article was written by Ted Levitt, a noted business scholar. It offers marketing advice that still rings true a generation after it was first published. But when it came to technological forecasting it fell victim to the Zeitgeist. It foresaw a bright future for ultrasonics: "Lurking in the wings and ready to make chemical dry cleaning totally obsolescent is that powerful magician, ultrasonics."[21] Apparently the only magic the magician was able to perform was a disappearing act.

Interestingly, in the 1960s there were many forecasts for the home dry cleaner. It was a logical extension of existing home appliances, such as the washer and dryer, present in the home at the time. But it never came to pass. Home dry cleaners are still unavailable. Commercial dry cleaning is still done with chemicals. Ultrasonics is not a force in this market or many others.

In fact, ultrasonics failed to serve most of the markets foreseen for it. Instead, it has served only small markets, such as cleaning jewelry and powering home humidifiers. Its most substantial market has been in hospitals to obtain images of internal organs. Contrary to expectations, dishwashers, showers, and other household appliances have been unaffected by developments in ultrasonics.

It should have been apparent beforehand that many of the intended uses for ultrasonics would never be. Even in the 1960s it should have been clear that water was not about to become obsolete for showering. It has inherent, if not archetypical, advantages over sound waves. "Being modern" was not about to change those behaviors. Ultrasonics illustrates the powerful, possibly even imprisoning, hold the Zeitgeist has on forecasters. It also illustrates how different the Zeitgeist of one period can be from the realities of another. An interesting question is: Are we falling into the same trap today with more modern, but equally unlikely, technologies? What many predict will change our lives in dramatic and far-reaching ways may really end up making only a modest mark.

Lest you think we now know better and are incapable of repeating those same errors for the same technology, consider a recent article in the *New York Times* that predicts a bright future for ultrasonics. Its title tells its emphasis: "Sound Is Shaped into a Dazzling Tool with Many Uses." According to experts, ultrasonics "are expected to spawn remarkable technologies in the next century." They will be used in superconducting and for levitating materials in midair. One expert laments, "It is much easier to do this in the microgravity of space than on earth." Ultrasonics will lead to the development of new materials based on new molecules. "In any case," this same expert predicts confidently, "ultrasonics is going to be one of the keys to our future."[22] We have heard it all before. It is likely that ultrasonics will continue to serve only micro-markets, whether or not they are produced in the microgravity of outer space.

Forecasts based on other specific technologies were also repeated in study after study, time and time again.

Plastics, which experienced explosive growth in the 1960s, were widely forecast as a principal component of housing. Instead, consumers prefer more traditional materials in the 1980s. A house with oak floors commands a higher price than one with plastic floors.

Modular housing was another popular forecast of the 1960s. Unfortunately, much of it fell apart, and housing aficionados have moved on to more traditional designs.

The tremendous expenditures to build the interstate system, which began in the 1950s, led to the widespread belief that the project would not be deemphasized after the sytem was nearly completed, but that it would be automated. Forecasts of this sort were common. In actuality, maintenance of the existing system has become a key issue of the 1980s.

These forecasts erred not by a matter of degree, they missed their target completely. The forecasters incorrectly assumed that the issues of the past would remain the issues of the future. Mostly, they were mistaken. They were overly influenced by the Zeitgeist, or the spirit of the times in which they lived.

6

Price-Performance Failures

Technological forecasts predicated on wild ideas and exotic technologies have no monopoly of failed forecasts. Forecasts for less elaborate products fail almost as often. Mostly, they fail because they espouse innovations that cost too much for the additional benefit they provide consumers.

A simple price-performance analysis would point out those shortcomings. It would show whether a proposed innovation is cost competitive with available alternatives.

The analysis does not have to be complex. Asking simple questions will go a long way toward avoiding the horrendous errors of the past, such questions as: What additional benefit does this product offer over existing entries? Will consumers have to, and be willing to, pay extra for it? Does the product offer a benefit over existing products that justifies a higher price?

It is amazing how often the proponents of a new product fail, or are unwilling, to ask those fundamental questions about the markets they seek to serve. Yet most of the innovations examined in this book would have handily failed a simple test that pitted benefits against costs. To be successful, new products, at the very least, must strike a subtle balance between the benefits they offer and the price that must be charged for them vis-à-vis competitive products. A failure to strike that balance usually means the new product will go nowhere, and the forecasts for it will fail.

Considering the cost-benefit position of the product in comparison with existing products is an essential ingredient of the forecast. Consumers will judge innovations against the way they currently do things. Higher prices must be commensurate with perceived additional benefits.

The linchpin of many cost-benefit comparisons is an estimate of how rapidly costs will decline as the market expands. Too often, those projections are overly optimistic. They assume that prices will drop dramatically as the market expands, but in many cases costs have declined more slowly than anticipated. Consequently, many new products have remained uncompetitive.

After-the-fact classifications of successful and failed forecasts are open to the criticism that such classifications are merely tautological. Some might argue that failed forecasts are classified as not striking a balance between costs and benefits simply because they failed. Successful forecasts are classified as striking the balance because they are successful. While there is no doubt many cases where cost-benefit comparisons are difficult to make beforehand, it is equally clear that many past forecasts failed because they were based on innovations that offered customers no benefit and, as a double-whammy, cost far more than what they were meant to replace. Exotic technologies will do this to you: They will cause you to lose all sense of economic reality. The true potential for those obvious examples, and many others, should have been apparent beforehand.

Furthermore, focusing on price-performance comparisons forces the forecaster to keep both feet firmly planted on the ground. Consider the following cases, and ask yourself whether it would not have been apparent that a failure was about to occur.

No Benefit for Consumers

Simply put, many forecasts call for a bright future for new products that offer customers no advantage over existing products. Not surprisingly, consumers do not bother to adopt them. While higher costs may be a partial reason why the products fail, it is not the main factor. The innovation fails because it offers benefits that were unwanted at any sensible price.

In the early 1960s many manufacturers felt that a new method for preserving foods was emerging: dehydration. Dehydrated foods would eliminate the need for refrigeration. Both Armour and Swift were working toward a "freeze-dried meat," and United

Fruit acquired a company that was selling freeze-dried shrimp. According to an Armour vice president, "We don't spend that kind of money unless we have confidence in the process."[1]

There were only two problems: The food did not taste very good, and the new process offered an advantage primarily to the manufacturer, who would rather not bother with all of that annoying refrigeration equipment. Consequently, dehydrated foods have penetrated only small markets for camping rations and beef jerky.

Like food in the form of pills and synthetic foods of all imaginable persuasions, predictions for dramatic advances in the things we eat have mostly fallen on their face. Consumers demand ever larger quantities of frozen foods, and other preparations that allow foods to be prepared conveniently, without the loss of natural tastes. But they do not desire to eliminate or bypass the eating experience. In fact, consumers are still willing to spend a hard day's pay on a sumptuous dinner that excites the senses and tastes delicious.

In 1972, quadraphonic stereo systems seemed to be the next logical step in a progression from mono to stereo phonographs. A CBS executive voiced the expectations of some in the industry when he predicted that sales would double to 1 million units in 1973 and grow to 3 million units in 1974 as four-channel systems replaced stereo "at an even faster rate than conversion to stereo."[2]

The trade was especially excited about the prospects for this innovation, because it meant that consumers would be purchasing four speakers instead of the usual two. Consumers were somewhat less excited. They perceived no dramatic enhancement in the quality of the sound as against existing stereo systems and were generally unwilling to pay the higher price.

What really hurt the innovation, however, were a lack of industry hardware standards and the limited selection of quadraphonic records. The product failed because competing manufacturers offered consumers incompatible formats, for which records were largely unavailable. Even if the product did offer a benefit, consumers were unable to realize it.

Manufacturers of compact disks, a similar innovation introduced a decade later, had learned an important lesson from quadraphonics. They purposely cooperated to install an industry-wide standard and ensured a steady supply of records. Further-more, they introduced the product to coincide with the robust economic recovery of 1983. What luck!

The videodisk is a well-known example of an innovation that failed to provide an incremental benefit over a competitive inno-vation, the VCR. The inability of the videodisk to record pro-grams for later playback ensured that the videodisk would fail while the VCR soared.

In 1972 Goodyear's Industrial Products Division thought it had identified a growing market for moving sidewalks. Its "Speedwalk" or "Speedramp" system would be used to transport shoppers and strollers around downtown areas, where no cars would be allowed. The firm felt confident that this would be a $6-billion-a-year industry in the 1980s. As one executive of the firm, ready for battle, put it "if our chunk is not $300-million, some tails will be chewed—especially mine."[3]

Needless to say, moving sidewalks did not turn out to be a growth market at all. In fact, large cities like New York spend huge sums to ensure that heaving sidewalks caused by freezing and thawing will not move unexpectedly and injure their citizens.

The prediction for moving sidewalks mistakenly assumed that there was a need for moving sidewalks and that cities would be willing to pay for them, neither of which turned out to be so. More important, a social trend emerged that recognized the healthful benefits of brisk walking. Once again, this prediction was in tune with the concept of "modern" in the 1960s but at odds with the realities of subsequent decades.

Designer tires was another innovation whose time never came. In the early 1960s Goodyear (the moving sidewalk people) tested a tire for passenger autos with a pastel-colored translucent sidewall. Inside the tire was a series of lightbulbs that would illuminate the tire. Safety was not the benefit, fashion was. A promotional brochure at the time asked: "Will the lady driver want tires to match her car's upholstery—or perhaps a favorite outfit?"[4] She wanted neither. In hindsight it seems incon-ceivable, but someone actually believed that people would want this product.

Finally, throughout the 1960s and early 1970s it was widely believed that "programmed learning" was an emerging educational market. The popularity of behaviorism and an infatuation with electronic gadgetry suggested that many persons would be educated by this method. Sales consistently lagged behind expectations. In hindsight, those machines were essentially expensive, electronic page-turners that offered few advantages over traditional methods of learning.

Interactive television also failed to catch fire, although it was widely expected to spawn a new dimension in television programming in the early 1980s. Warner Communications teamed up with American Express to form Warner Amex Cable Communications Inc., which offered QUBE service, which allowed subscribers to "talk back" to their television. For an additional monthly fee, viewers could engage in all sorts of exciting entertainment: They could respond to opinion polls, answer questions of interest to advertisers, and purchase goods at home by pressing a button on the box. (Children turned out to be especially interested in ordering this way, much to the chagrin of their parents. A $350 moped was a favorite item among the kids. But when a deliveryman showed up at the door with the product and the bill for it, parents saw fewer benefits to interactive home cable TV shopping. Fortunately QUBE took returns.)

At first, consumers in the Columbus, Ohio, test market seemed to enjoy the service and participated vigorously. As time passed, however, the newness of the service faded, and consumers reverted to their old preference for passive entertainment—inactive, if not interactive, TV provided the better benefit. Warner Amex pulled the plug on QUBE service in the mid-1980s.

QUBE's failure went unheeded. Only a few years later, in 1987, toymakers pursued what they considered to be a major growth market—toys, games, and movies that interacted with TV viewers. It was called "the next generation of interactive products." Hadn't anyone bothered to look back to see that the first generation had passed away at a young age?

Mattel entered with "Captain Power," in which kids shot at TV bad guys. Hasbro was working on interactive videos, which allowed viewers to choose their own plot lines. Worlds of Wonder was developing mysteries and football games with changeable outcomes. That was only the beginning. Soon adults would be competing in quiz shows from home and pressing their way to happiness. As one expert noted, "The time has come when people will have the choice of watching *Raiders of the Lost Ark,* or being in *Raiders of the Lost Ark.*"[5] Some were skeptical, but most manufacturers were afraid of missing out on the next "moneyboat," as one consultant called it. The boat never sailed. Mystery movies with different outcomes, like Clue, proved unsuccessful. More elaborate schemes never had a chance. The reasons were clear. Some interactive products required consumers to purchase hundreds of dollars' worth of equipment to interact with their TVs, including videodisks, which had failed badly a few years earlier. More important, research done at the time indicated key findings about the market the manufacturers intended to serve with these wondrous products: Viewers liked to be entertained passively and do not like to press buttons. In the end, viewers did not want more control over their TVs. They wanted to be entertained.

A more recent example is videotex, widely hailed as a growth market in the early 1980s. It has penetrated the French market—although the French have heavily subsidized the technology. In the United States it has gone nowhere. Most consumers have no strong desire to manipulate checking accounts electronically or scan data bases in their spare time. And they are certainly unwilling to pay a hefty fee for the equipment necessary to do so. Meanwhile, providers of those services search tirelessly for a service that consumers will find beneficial.

It is often hard to see the benefit offered by at least some of the high technology predicted as part of the car of the future. A recent version of the Cadillac Voyage, the sedan of the 1990s, had no rearview mirror.[6] Instead, it came equipped with a backward-looking camera in the trunk and a TV screen in the dashboard. Another dash-mounted TV screen housed the inertial navigation system, which continuously plotted the car's position. A simple price-performance analysis would ask whether those innovations are superior to a silver-backed mirror mounted on a bracket and a paper map stored in the glove compartment (for which consumers still resist paying 75 cents), both of which are clearly cheaper. Furthermore, older consumers, the ones who buy Cadillac cars in the first place, are less interested in technological wizardry and less likely to pay for it.

GM's infrared night vision device is also likely to meet its maker shortly. Based on the benefit that drivers overdrive their headlights, this wonder places yet another TV screen on the dash, this one with "menu controls." Using the system, night drivers would be able to see through rain, snow, fog, and smoke. The device has only a few drawbacks. For one, it requires a huge roof-mounted box to contain the system. Furthermore, it requires cooling with liquid nitrogen to 70 degrees above absolute zero![7] Sensibly, Ford and Chrysler are not pursuing the technology. They consider it impractical.

The computerphone, a recent innovation which married the data processing capabilities of the personal computer to the voice and data communications capabilities of the modern telephone, has also failed to excite consumer interest, although initial expectations for the product were high. Entrepreneurial firms such as Zaisan Corp. introduced reasonably priced, powerful computerphones in 1984. Other firms followed. It was expected to be a classic case of large firms following smaller pioneers into the market.

The market for computerphones was expected to reach $1 billion a year within a few years. In 1984 *Business Week* reported: "Most analysts are predicting fast growth in the computer-phone market."[8] Most experts were wrong. The market never materialized. The makers of the machines were unable to convince business buyers that they needed the product. A PC with a modern modem seemed to do the job just fine. A sales pitch that argued that the computerphone eliminated desktop clutter proved unpersuasive. Less than a year later *Business Week* reexamined the computerphone market. One computer retailer reflecting on his lack of success selling the product notes: "People see it as an expensive PC with a phone on it—with no need for it."[9] Others felt that computerphone manufacturers had not really figured out what the market wanted. Such severe shortcomings are likely to dampen enthusiasm for the product for years to come.

Even the emergence of new sports can fail because of missing benefits. In 1985 the *New York Times* analyzed the decline and demise of professional soccer in the United States. At the time, both the North American Soccer League (NASL) and the Major Indoor Soccer League (MISL) were about to go under (they eventually did.) Soccer, it seems, does not offer a large benefit to Americans. The *Times* concluded, "Soccer is not a commodity, it comes with a 100-year history of intense human involvement. It is a sport that seems to call for a peculiarly intimate and passionate involvement with its fans. But there is no such thing as instant involvement."[10] Indeed there was not. Americans were bored by the low scores and stayed away from the games. The *Times* concludes that Sam Goldwyn was right when he stated: "If they don't wanna come, you can't stop them."

Too Expensive

Some innovations provide a recognizable benefit over existing products, but the benefit is not enough to justify a higher price. Hence, these innovations serve much smaller markets than originally intended, where costs are less important.

A serious disregard for costs was a particular problem for the technological forecasts made during the heady days of the 1960s when the economy boomed throughout most of the decade and it was a national goal to place a man on the moon by the end of the decade—regardless of the cost. Predictions were colored greatly by the spirit of the times. No one seemed to be willing to ask such simple questions as, Who will pay for these fantastic inventions? Is there any need for them? Is there really a market for undersea motels and factories? Who are the potential customers? Will people want to live in plastic houses? As noted by the authors of the TRW "Probe" study examined in a previous chapter, "in today's economy, cost seems of secondary importance if the project is worthwhile."[11] In the 1960s, advances in technology held sway over less flamboyant, but more practical, concerns.

Asking sensible questions about the costs and benefits of innovation projects is not an arcane proposal, but it is a proposal that is often not made. Many forecasts still call for fantastic, outrageously expensive projects without regard for the accompanying costs. Frank Davidson, for example, is an extreme case. "Wealth is a result of engineering," he says; "it does not spring full born like Pegasus from Medusa's blood, out of a science of economics." He argues further: "More of the engineering mentality must enter into the old liberal professions."[12] He advocates many break-the-bank ideas, including a tunnel under the North Atlantic, beaming energy back to earth from space stations, and offshore cities! The tunnel would reduce pollution, stabilize transportation prices, and save many dollars now spent on shipbuilding and airplanes. The enormous cost of the project seems not to be an important concern. As Davidson points out, "The world has entered an era where its engineering abilities far outstrip its traditional experience in analysis and organization."

Fortunately, the nation has not outstripped its common sense. Some government decision-makers still value price-performance comparisons. In 1987 Congress was still asking whether a minimum expenditure of $12 billion for a space station first proposed back in the mid-1960s, around the time of the TRW study, is prudent given the possible return. The space expert John Pike of the Federation of American Scientists recently observed: "The big question about the space station is whether there will be a demand or whether they will just sit up there playing cards and measuring each other's heartbeats."[13] It is a good question worthy of a satisfactory answer. The proponents of this project may well be committing a common error: pursuing a project with a wanton disregard for the costs it carries.

Graphite fibers offer another example. In 1970 they were widely hailed as a lightweight replacement for the metals used to reinforce structural parts in airplanes and other products where weight is an important factor. The material has the strength of steel at one-fifth the weight. However, in 1970 it carried a heavy price tag—almost $400 a pound. The industry knew of that cost disadvantage but believed it could be reduced to $25 a pound by 1980. As a result, an executive of Union Carbide predicted, "In ten years it could be a $100 million business."[14] That assumption was overly optimistic. DuPont's Kevlar, once hailed as the next Nylon, has been able to crack only small markets, such as bullet-proof vests, the modern-day suits of armor.

Another example is foam-filled tires. In 1968, Dow Corning thought it had found a superior substitute for air-filled tires that would eventually penetrate the consumer automotive market. The tiremakers were skeptical because of the greater cost and weight of this tire. Dow Corning was convinced that "in time its new technology will make believers out of present nonbelievers."[15] It attracted few converts. The tires remain puncture-proof. The market remains flat.

The "forever" light bulb has yet to replace regular bulbs in the household market, even though it offers a distinct benefit. With normal daily usage it can be expected to burn for fifty years, or 80,000 hours. The three industry giants—GE, GTE, and North American Philips—hold roughly 90 percent of the regular light bulb market. They are not worried about this supposed innovation. They still prefer to sell regular bulbs that burn for a measly 1,000 hours. Why? It seems the "forever" bulb burns dimmer and costs much more. Consequently, most consumers still prefer to replace their bulbs as they burn out rather than to buy a single bulb that will last a virtual lifetime.[16]

In 1972 plastic paper, a substitute for pulp-based paper, cost about twice what pulp-based paper did, but it was predicted "that the price curves are going to cross as early as 1980."[17] That estimate proved to be overly optimistic, given the run-up in petroleum prices, the feedstock for plastics.

One of the most stunning failures of high technology was AT-&T's picture telephone. Although expectations for the product were high, and many experts considered it a near certainty that the innovation would revolutionize many markets, it has so far served very few customers after years of intense effort. The company had been working on the product since at least the 1930s. The invention of the transistor in 1948 allowed the product to be reduced to a more manageable size. Commercial service was to begin in 1964, the same year the product was featured at the New York World's Fair.

The advantages of the picture phone were clear. You could meet face to face with customers and colleagues without the expense and bother of business travel. On the long term, electronic meetings would render personal meetings obsolete. Ultimately, the picture phone would serve the home market, where household callers could not only speak but speak and be seen.

With the picture telephone, salesmen would travel electronically rather than physically. They could literally see their customers without leaving their desks. Productivity would increase while travel expenses declined. Besides, according to one expert, central business districts were dispersing. Soon it would be difficult for cities to support public transportation.

Other advantages would also accrue to users. With a keyboard they could tie into mainframe computers and work out problems at their desks. The picture phone would also serve as a precursor to videotex. Customers could view airline reservations, stock quotations, and a host of other databases.

Picture phone service was installed at Union Carbide as a test. The company loved it. It cut down on interoffice visits and kept business meetings on business topics.

World's Fair visitors were awed by the picture phone. So were the forecasters. A 1969 article in *The Bell Laboratories Record* noted that "just as the telephone has revolutionized human habits of communicating and made a major contribution to the quality of human life, many of us at Bell Labs believe that PIC-TUREPHONE service, the service that lets people see as well as hear each other, offers potential benefits to mankind of the same magnitude."[18] Advertisements in the business press of the late 1960s announced the product's features and pictured the desktop model.[19] It was predicted that there would be 100,000 picturephones in use by 1975. By the1980s "these phones would be widely used by the general public—perhaps replacing some forms of transportation, such as trips to local stores to examine merchandise before making purchases."[20] Study after study predicted the same opportunities for the picture telephone.

A study entitled "A Long Look Ahead," conducted for AT&T by the Institute for the Future in mid-1969, proved no exception. Big changes were in store for AT&T. "The world of 1985," the study warned, "will be markedly different from today's."[21] There would be 3 million picture telephones in use in the United States, generating revenues of $5 billion. Other radical changes would occur. Telephone communications would increase because street violence would be so bad that citizens would fear traveling. By 1985 there was about a fifty-fifty chance "that riots and guerrilla warfare incidents will be common in at least one of the major cities at any given time" (p. 7). The study saw many changes, including changes in the regulatory climate. Regulatory agencies would be increasingly involved in goal-setting, for example. Luckily, regulatory agencies would permit rate increases to permit growth. But, according to the study, "AT&T participation in unregulated business is unlikely." Nearly every prediction was dead wrong. Furthermore, the study failed to foresee the biggest event in the history of AT&T—the breakup of the company. In exchange for the right to enter unregulated businesses, it agreed to be broken up.

What happened to the picture telephone was far different from what was predicted. Customers may have been awed by the product but they were also awed by its price. When it came to paying for the service they decided to forgo the video portion of the product. They decided to just listen rather than look and listen.

The product was not killed, however. In the early 1980s it evolved into the Picturephone meeting service. Special rooms were set up where "leading edge" companies could hold face-to-face meetings without actually meeting face to face. Mostly, the service offered the same benefits as those offered nearly twenty years earlier.

The meeting service met mostly with failure. Video teleconferencing never made a dent in business travel. Other business services offered by AT&T soared while picturephone service slumped. Pressing the flesh proved insurmountably superior to pressing buttons. John Naisbitt's contention that high technology leads to a higher demand for personal contact, what he calls "high touch," certainly rings true in the case of the picturephone.[22]

The advantages of the picturephone over ordinary telephone service were questionable and surely expensive. In the early 1970s some blamed a recession for the product's slow start. But the product's problems lay deeper. Post-mortems usually attribute the product's demise to high initial costs. But high costs alone did not destroy the picturephone. What really killed it was that it offered a benefit that was awesome and amusing but essentially unwanted. There is little need to see a person over the phone for perfunctory personal and business communications. Furthermore, in situations where personal contact is crucial, seeing people over the phone is a poor substitute for meeting them in person. Consequently, the video phone was really competing with the traditional telephone, not "in-the-flesh" meetings. Furthermore, the traditional audio telephone proved to be a more than sufficient medium. Sensibly and successfully, that is where the emphasis is now placed. Enhancing the audio telephone has led to cost-effective benefits and profitable services. The lack of benefits for the picture telephone over the voice-only telephone, coupled with the much higher price that had to be charged for the service, disconnected the prospects for this technological product.

The case of cellular telephones, another expensive innovation, but one that has proved a success, reinforces this conclusion. Car phones do not replace travel, they enhance its usefulness. They expand on an existing base of usage. They also possess the coveted cachet of snob appeal, unlike CB radios, which also aid mobile communications but carry a distinctly downscale image. Consequently, the market for cellular phones has grown quickly, to $600 million in 1986. As prices drop, demand is expected to climb further.

Changing Benefits

Sometimes innovations do offer consumers a desired benefit, but consumers later change their minds and demand a new and different benefit. The manufacturer is then left with an unwanted product that offers an obsolete benefit.

Turning fuel into food is one of the most absurd examples of how the benefits demanded from a product can change dramatically within only a few years. In 1967 the *Wall Street Journal* reported that the major oil companies were seeking to expand the market for their products. One promising opportunity was the conversion of fuel into food. Gulf scientists were turning petroleum into cookies, soups, and cereals. Standard Oil of New Jersey had teamed up with Nestlé to enter the so-called "oil food field." This market looked promising because of the overabundance of inexpensive oil and natural gas, and the population explosion. Supporters of the market opportunity thought the only problem to be overcome was psychological: convincing consumers that there was nothing wrong with ingesting petroleum-based products. At least one oil-producing nation felt so strongly about the prospects for this market they sought to conserve their oil reserves for conversion into food to feed a hungry populace.

An official of the Mexican oil monopoly, Petroleos Mexicanos, noted, "You wouldn't burn wheat, would you? Petroleum has more protein content than wheat."[23] Ironically, less than a decade later there was a preponderance of predictions calling for exactly that—the conversion of foodstocks into ethanol.

The lessons of this humorous error are instructive. It failed because it was predicated on the erroneous assumptions that oil would remain abundant and inexpensive and that its products could be made appetizing. Furthermore, interest shifted from feeding the world's hungry to fueling the world's cars.

The automobile industry has been especially hard hit by the problem of shifting benefits. Mostly, this can be attributed to the on-again, off-again supply problems of the 1970s, which whipsawed consumers' demands for industry's products. Consider the following examples.

Diesel-powered cars were extremely popular right after the second oil crisis in 1979, and with good reason—diesel fuel was cheaper than gasoline, the cars got better mileage, and they were more reliable owing to fewer moving parts. Consumers wanted efficiency, and the diesel provided it. They willingly paid a premium on the sticker price and waited months for delivery to have a diesel.

Detroit automakers sold a whopping 500,000 diesel cars in 1981, the peak year. But it was all downhill from there. Gas became cheaper than diesel fuel, and consumers found the cars to be dirty and temperamental. The craze for the diesel turned into a bust.[24]

Further attacks on the internal combusion engine failed just as resoundingly, but for different reasons. This has made predicting changes in the auto industry an especially unrewarding exercise.

In the 1960s the internal combustion engine was attacked as a polluter. A great effort was expended to find a superior alternative. One contender was Bill Lear's "steam-powered" car—an update of the old Stanley Steamer, which had challenged the internal combustion engine earlier in the century. It had two distinct advantages. It burned remarkably clean, with few pollutants, and was invented by a man with an excellent record of previous technological developments and commercial success (the Learjet, the automobile tape deck).

In 1971 Bill Lear predicted: "Within ten years, the internal-combustion engine will be a collector's item."[25] His prediction was supported by an opinion poll of 411 scientists in 1968 indicating that 63 percent believed the steam car would be mass-produced in the near future.[26]

The steam car had only one disadvantage, it got horrible gas mileage, which was inherent in its design. Consequently, it died with the first energy crunch. Lear lamented in 1974, "The emphasis changed from pollution control to fuel conservation."[27]

Another challenger to the internal combustion engine was General Motors' and Mazda's rotary engine. The rotary engine possessed the advantage of fewer moving parts. It incorporated some rather innovative principles and appeared to have a bright future. In 1971, a Mazda executive predicted that the company would sell 500,000 rotary engines a year by 1975.[28] It sold far fewer.

During the 1960s and 1970s American auto producers were widely criticized for not being innovative enough. Critics argued that Detroit was wedded to the internal combustion engine even though other engine designs were superior. Unfortunately, when some manufacturers attempted to change they got burned. The critics disappeared with the times, leaving the automakers holding a bag of usually worthless innovations.

As a group, those innovations in the auto industry failed because the market-place demanded a new benefit different from the one that had been planned for. Consumers, and Government policy, called for cars that got good gas mileage. By some unfortunate stroke of fate, innovative engines provided terrible gas mileage; they were perfectly suited for a market that no longer existed.

Oddly, it was predicted that small cars would dominate the U.S. auto market long before the energy crisis hit. Typical is the 1970 forecast by a Volkswagen VP: "By 1980 I can see no big cars around."[29] A British Leyland executive voiced a similar opinion. Those predictions were not motivated by fuel economy. The oil crisis was still some years away. Instead, the large car had become a symbol of American excessiveness and wastefulness. It also polluted the air, a key concern at the time.

Ironically, what the British Leyland executive failed to see was that the small cars manufactured by his firm (MG, Triumph) would be withdrawn from the U.S. market because, although they were small, they managed to get poor gas mileage—a difficult feat of engineering perfected by his firm.

The auto industry has been whipsawed by demand for changes for more than a decade. It seems that when they make small cars, consumers want large cars, and vice versa. It is difficult to excel, and easy to criticize, when the demands of consumers change so rapidly.

Longer-term automotive trends have also been set on end. In 1979 an article in *Smithsonian* reviewed past forecasts and asked "Whatever became of the predicted effortless world?"[30] It found that although we were supposed to be living in a world of automated wonder, actual changes had been far more modest. Sam Love, the author, points to Futurama, the Depression-era GM exhibit at the 1939 World's Fair as one example. It foresaw automated highway systems that operated with incredible precision. It also foresaw a continued trend in the speed of autos. By 1960, it was predicted, highway speeds would reach 100 miles per hour. It was a reasonable extrapolation, but it turned out to be wrong. Until 1939 auto speed had been increasing steadily. Surely technological advances would continue to make cars faster. The issues that changed the trend—the oil crisis and concerns for highway safety—were not apparent in the 1930s.

In 1967 the *Wall Street Journal* looked at the future of the automobile as part of a series it called "Shape of the Future." The article was titled: "Concern over Pollution and Safety Will Force Major Changes in Cars."[31] The report nicely sums up the prominent beliefs of the day, most of which turned out to have little to do with the future.

Pollution and safety were the paramount issues of the late 1960s. Critics of the auto industry were everywhere. The automobile was perceived as the cause of many perceived maladies of the day. It seemed that the future of the automobile would be largely determined by pollution and safety issues. Future technology would be brought to bear on those problems. Electric cars and turbine engines would reduce pollution levels. Cars would be made safer by automatic steering, braking, and acceleration systems. It was all part of a larger scheme to computerize traffic control and automate highways. But not in large cities. Soon cars would be banned from city streets. Mass transit would boom. Those were all popular predictions of the late 1960s. They all made sense at the time.

Auto experts had a different vision. Cars would continue to proliferate as the number of cars per family continued to increase. In fact, future cars would be designed for specialized tasks. A small electric-powered "shopper" would be used by families for short hauls. It would have three wheels, only two seats, and a single door that opened from the front. Families would also have a "cruiser" with automatic controls for intercity travel. Car–boat combinations equipped with retractable wheels would be popular for recreation on both roads and water. Five-car garages would be common, sometimes taking over the entire first floor of suburban homes.

Radical changes were in store for the auto of the future. Aerodynamics would increasingly be incorporated into car design—a clear, but rare, hit in hindsight. But windows would be sealed permanently, leaving air-conditioning as the sole source of ventilation. That is the way it was done on jets.

Controls would also change radically. Traditional steering wheels would be replaced by two smaller wheels, one for each hand. GM was working a unistick design—push to accelerate, pull to brake, turn by moving side to side. Many of those innovations would first appear as optional equipment. That would give customers a chance to unlearn ingrained habits.

Computerized highways were certain to be the wave of the future. Even the government was enamored of computer control. An official at the Bureau of Public Roads foresaw that "you'll see more emphasis on computers than concrete" (p. 10). A recent ride on the interstate verifies the accuracy of his prediction: Potholes aplenty await the unwary motorist. Hang on to the unistick, the cruiser is about to hit a pothole. Henry Ford II saw similar visions:

In the future we foresee the possible development of a nationwide traffic control system based on Earth survey satellites or aerial reconnaissance linked by computer to urban traffic control centers and finally to the stop sign on the corner and then to the radio in your car. As fantastic as it may seem, we believe such a system will be technically feasible and economically sound.[p. 10]

It was fantastic, but it was also impractical. The system turned out to be an unwise expenditure of taxpayers' money.

Economics killed most of those innovations. Automated highways equipped with "seeing" devices embedded either in highways or cars never made it. As observed in 1967, such a system would be outrageously expensive. Furthermore, there was no fair way to keep older cars off the automated highways.

Predictions called for 100,000 electric cars by 1975. Unless golf carts are counted, the actual amount fell far short of that predicted. Electric cars proved uncompetitive with traditional designs. Better battery designs never materialized. Even after the run-up of fuel prices in the 1970s and numerous performance improvements, batteries were never cost competitive.

Turbine engines were widely touted in 1967. Turbines cut pollution significantly. Unfortunately, they were voracious gas guzzlers and had an acceleration lag. Press on the pedal of a turbine car, and nothing happens. Six seconds later the car takes off. As one official noted: "This would make crossing a busy intersection a really sporting proposition" (p. 10). Still, Ford foresaw bright visions for the turbine car. One expert said that by 1985 "there will be a lot of gas turbines around" (p. 10). It never happened. Most of those innovations disappeared with the constant flow of new issues that have affected the auto industry. Remarkably, today's autos have deep roots in past designs. In fact, technological changes have been evolutionary, not revolutionary.

Finally, no-frill foods, or generics, also turned out to be a trend that soared, then soured. In the mid-1970s West Germany's Albrecht Group opened the first no-frills supermarket in the Midwest. The store eliminated bagging, check-cashing, and other expensive services. Instead, it offered customers prices that were 20 percent lower than at traditional supermarkets. Jewel supermarkets quickly followed by selling generics in their stores. Then the crowd entered. The market for no-frill foods exploded. Customers and retailers alike were interested in price. Experts uniformly predicted that generics would continue to grow rapidly, shifting the balance of power from the manufacturers of national brands to retailers. This contrasted greatly with earlier predictions, which uniformly held that generics had no future.

Warehouse stores, which offered customers lower prices, proved to be a related fad. Many experts saw visions of repeating patterns. As one expert noted: "We are coming back full circle to the bare-bones approach of the original supermarket."[32]

The circle closed only briefly. Generics and warehouse stores faded with the economic recovery of 1983. All of a sudden, consumers decided that no-frill products were undesirable. As quickly as it all began, it all ended. What had begun as a consumer-driven market ended the same way. Instead of a growth market it turned out to be a fad. It went straight up and straight down. Whether consumer interest will return with the next economic downturn is a matter of conjecture.

7

Demographic, Social, and Political Trends

Some forecasts fail because they mistakenly assume the continuation of a long-standing demographic, social, or political trend. Often the opposite has occurred. Long-term trends can shift suddenly and unexpectedly.

Mistaken Demographic Trends

In the past, many forecasts have failed because they were predicated on demographic forecasts that turned out to be badly mistaken. More often, the implications of population trends were misread. In the 1960s, for example, the population was exploding. Imminent food shortages and world hunger were prominent concerns of the day. In 1966 the *Wall Street Journal* examined population trends and the changes they would bring. By the year 2000 the population of the earth was expected to be double that of 1966. There would be 6 billion people on the planet. How would we feed all those people? it was asked. The Malthusian nightmare seemed finally to be reaching fulfillment.

The United States would not be spared. Our country was in the midst of a baby boom. Since World War II, Americans had reproduced themselves at an alarming rate. Clearly, the experts assumed, the trend would continue. The baby-boomers would imitate the reproductive patterns of its parents. There were so many of them, however, that as they approached the prime childbearing age the population would explode. According to Census Bureau predictions the U.S. population would reach 263 million by 1985, 340 million by the year 2000. In 1966 the population was only 198 million. Rapid growth was expected.

In constructing those forecasts the Census Bureau mistakenly assumed that American women would have an average of 3.1 children each.

Continued growth meant that the age breakdown of the future U.S. population would not change much: 40 percent would still be under twenty, 51 percent between twenty and sixty-four, and only 9 percent would be over sixty-four.

In the United States, population growth would lead to many problems. For one, people would continue to move from rural areas to cities. Population density would soar.

The director of Harvard University's Center for Population Studies predicted that there would not be enough coastline for recreational purposes. His recommendation: "Build artificial offshore islands for 21st Century ocean bathers."[1]

His estimates were greatly colored by the confluence of two important trends of the day: population growth and increased automation. Those two trends would greatly increase the leisure time of Americans. In the 1960s, that was a popular opinion.

In actuality the baby boom ended with the 1960s. Careers, contraception, abortion, and the economic burden of bearing many offspring deterred couples from having large families. Instead of 3.1 children, the average woman had 2.1 children in 1976, and the figure declined into the 1980s. For many Americans, quality of life took precedence over the quantity of life.

As a result, the U.S. population will not reach 340 million by the year 2000. Instead, it is more likely to reach the predicted level for 1985—263 million. In 1986 there were 241 million people living in the United States.

The end of the baby boom increased the percentage of older people. By the year 2000 the baby boom will be beginning to move into their fifties. The United States is growing older.

By 1976 the outlook had changed. The migration to cities ended. In fact, it reversed. So had opinions regarding large urban area. Many experts now asked whether cities were obsolete. Why? Advances in communications had lessened the need for face-to-face meetings. Innovations like teleconferencing had a brighter future than cities. Rural areas now grew faster than cities.

Older cities in the North faced a bleak future. New York had just gone bankrupt. According to the president of a large relocation firm, New York City would lose half its jobs by the year 2000. Bad times lay ahead.

Sun belt cities would grow fastest. The three cities with the brightest prospects were Denver, Dallas, and Houston. Times had changed. But not for long. In the 1980s trends turned again. The forecast for those "bright spots" proved short-lived. Denver and Houston had the highest office vacancy rates in the United States throughout most of the 1980s. In 1976, who would have guessed that the Northeast would grow vigorously while Texas tumbled?

Tempered forecasts that called for more modest changes again performed best. In a follow-up report in 1976, the *Wall Street Journal* recognized that there would be "no futuristic cityscape." In fact, "In their physical appearance, cities are expected to change far less by the year 2000 than was predicted in this newspaper and elsewhere 10 years ago."[2]

In 1959, Crane Brinton, writing in the *New York Times,* also tried his hand at demographic predictions.[3] Most forecasts called for a continued boom in the U.S. population—a simple extrapolation of then current trends. Brinton took a different tack. He correctly predicted a turning point by 1970, with small families of one or two children. He focused on the economic consequences of choosing to have a large family. He was right. The birthrate began to decline in the 1960s.

Brinton errs only when he deviates from his own philosophy. He predicts that by 1970 the pendulum would swing back to where it had been in the early 1900s: to small families accompanied by a return to Victorian sexual repression in the populace. In reality, that turned out to be wishful thinking. The pendulum swung to small families, but the sexual excesses of the 1960s turned out to be anything but Victorian.

In the late 1950s, while the postwar baby boom was well under way, many population forecasts simply projected then current birth trends into the future. Consequently, most population forecasts made at that time overshot their target.

James Bylin, writing in the *Wall Street Journal,* reviewed previous population forecasts made in the 1950s and published in popular magazines.[4] Relying on "conservative" estimates *Reader's Digest* pegged the U.S. population at 208 million by 1970. Alaska would grow the most, climbing from 225,000 to 500,000 by 1970. *U.S. News and World Report* predicted the U.S. population would reach 210 million. Allen Nevins, predicting for the *New York Times*, also foresaw 210 million.

But by 1970 the baby boom had ended and the birthrate had slowed. In 1970, the target year, the U.S. population reached only 203 million. Alaska's population reached only 280,000.

Shifting Social Trends

Predicting social trends is one of the most difficult forecasts to make. Social trends involve people, who, unlike physical quantities, do not behave according to physical laws. Instead they change often, and in unpredictable ways. As a result, forecasts of social trends are notoriously inaccurate.

In the permissive 1960s, for example, who would have predicted that a conservative President would be overwhelmingly elected in 1980? Radical college students in the 1960s saw a revolution in this country as a real possibility. In the 1980s, those same persons flocked to business schools and coveted highly paid careers in investment banking. Will they be farmers in the 1990s? Or will they shift back to the left?

A measurement example best illustrates the difference between physical objects and human beings. If the length, width, and height of a desk are measured with a ruler, then the desk is shipped to Bombay, India, and the measurement repeated, the result will be the same. If you repeat the measure a year later it will remain the same.

Contrast this example with measurement of people's opinions and beliefs. If you ask a person his or her opinion, come back a month later, and repeat the question, you may get a different answer.

Furthermore, different social pressures are likely to elicit different opinions. Surveys of TV viewing and newspaper readership are likely to elicit inflated percentages of persons who watch public television and read the *New York Times* and *Wall*

Street Journal. Conversely, understimates of pornography viewership and the reading of lurid tabloids are likely.

In his December 1969 review, James Bylin also evaluated the accuracy of forecasts that contained social trends. He concluded that most of the forecasts turned out to be wrong. They missed the Vietnam War, the civil rights movement, the drug culture, and the permissive life-styles of the 1960s.

Changing Times, for example, predicted that by 1970 the growing number of teenagers, affected by the trend toward affluence, would be more "clothes conscious than their elders." That would lead to "a big decade for sportswear and dress-up clothing" (p.12). In the 1960s affluence led large numbers of teenagers to overindulgence rather than conspicuous consumption in clothing.

Some predictions of growth markets failed to consider the effect of changing demographics and social trends on their product entries. Laredo cigarettes, a "roll-your-own" brand, was less expensive than more traditional brands. According to a Brown & Williamson executive, the product fitted nicely with its price-based historical strategy: "It's a natural extension of the idea we've been pursuing since the 1930s." It was also less appealing to most consumers. Cost was not an important attribute sought by younger consumers. More important, in most social settings, smoking "roll-your-own" cigarettes conveyed an image of Depression-era poverty, an indigent derelict, or an ardent marijuana smoker. Consumers decided that smoking roll-your-own cigarettes was bad for their image. Consequently, with the exception of those who coveted an alternate lifestyle, consumers passed the product by.

Small cigars, like Tijuana Smalls, which were widely advertised in the early 1970s, also faced changing social mores. The cigars were targeted to the burgeoning young male segment. One firm's advertisements even asked whether you should offer a Tiparillo to a lady. One executive stated, "We firmly believe that small cigars of this type are the wave of the future."[5] Consumers did not agree. Since 1975, sales of small cigars have declined precipitously even though the number of young males skyrocketed.

Large cigars—with the exception of the very high end of the market—have suffered a similar fate. It is a product that is losing touch with the times. Sales of cigars have moved steadily downward. Apparently, men have decided to pursue other vices. Whereas cigars had once been widely considered a sign of wealth and success, they are now perceived mostly as a dirty habit with clear negative health consequences. Furthermore, the perception of cigar smoking in most social settings is quickly moving into the same category as spitting—a popular practice of years past. Instead of offering a Tiparillo to a lady, as was advocated by a popular ad campaign of more than fifteen years ago, men have given up smoking in record numbers. Most women would just as soon spit as smoke a cigar in the late 1980s.

Cigarettes seem to be facing a similar fate. Some forecasters believe that by the year 2000 cigarette smoking will have the cachet that chewing and spitting has today. Remember, spitting was a popular practice earlier in this century. It fell out of favor with most members of the populace. The few renegades who still engage in the habit probably represent the main market for roll-your-own cigarettes.

Similarly, in the late 1960s there was a belief that as the baby-boomers reached drinking age there would be a growing market for scotch whisky. After all, Scotch had been the drink of choice for their parents. It was felt that Scotch would also be the "in drink" among the young, upscale members of the baby-boom segment. It was not. Those consumers preferred less harsh-tasting spirits. As a result, vodka and tequila boomed, while scotch has stagnated at the same level since 1972. In this case, the demographics were right, but the behavior was unexpected.

Political Decisions

Politics played a role in the outcome of some forecasts. A concern in the late 1960s was for the tremendous surplus that was accumulating in the Social Security fund. It was warned that if something was not done, the system would literally by swamped by a tidal wave of money. Politicians eagerly tackled and solved that onerous problem. *Business Week* reported: "The administration has offered to attack the problem of the surplus from all sides. It would boost benefits, expand the program, and switch more revenue to coverage of rising hospital costs."[6]

Some might say that they went too far. The program now struggles to remain solvent. Younger workers, when polled, consistently report that they expect the system will be unable to meet their retirement needs. The experts state that without some fundamental change in the system, they are right.

In the mid-1960s government spending combined with a love of technological gadgetry, unfettered optimism, and a huge number of students progressing through the public school system led to expected revolutions in education. In August 1966 *Fortune* published an article entitled "Technology Is Knocking at the Schoolhouse Door." Schools would soon enter their own version of the industrial revolution. It was an idea whose time was overdue. As one expert noted: "Public education is the last great stronghold of the manual trades."[7] Industry would transform education through technological wonder.

The impetus was Lyndon Johnson's "creative federalism." Specifically, the Elementary and Secondary Education Act of 1965 provided large federal grants for schools to buy gadgets galore and to conduct research into alternative education programs. The buyers and researchers who soaked up the money were amazingly productive.

Educational leaders began by reforming the entire curriculum. It was warned: "This has *not* meant a return to McGuffey's readers or The Great Books, however" (p.123). Instead, we had entered a new age. According to this analysis, much of the knowledge students needed to excel in the future has not even been discovered yet! Furthermore, much of the traditional sort of thing being taught in schools was obsolete and irrelevant. Films, laboratories, and creative programs of every ilk would provide a modern alternative.

Some educators even argued for a new concept of intelligence. Schools were viewed as artificial institutions that stood in the way of the child's innate desire to learn. Abolishing schools was a radical idea even at the time, but some influential educators thought it might be a good one.

The "discovery method" of learning had wider support among educators. This pedagogical tool showed students the facts and had them draw their own conclusions. Is it any wonder that students have not the vaguest notion where Toronto is?

Individualized instruction, letting students learn at their own pace, was an honorable, and widely held, goal. Enter computers and programmed learning. Edison Responsive Environment's Talking Typewriter was one wonder. It used the principle of feedback from Skinnerian behaviorism to teach children the alphabet. IBM's 1500 system relied on recorded sound messages, light pens, typewriters, and buttons a-plenty.

All of those advances were incompatible with the old-fashioned organization of schools by grade. It was clear which would go. When the advances were implemented, "new knowledge about learning and new teaching technologies will expand our capacity to learn by several orders of magnitude" (p. 205).

It is fascinating to observe that nearly twenty-five years later exactly the opposite has occurred in education. The newfangled methods turned out to be naïvely idealistic. They did not work, much less increase learning by several magnitudes. "The Great Books" are once again back in fashion, as are the three Rs stressed by basic readers. Furthermore, teaching technology turned out to be too expensive for the benefit it provided. Even forgetting about the bankruptcy of the ideas themselves, the right questions were being asked. Speaking of elaborate teaching technologies, one lone voice noted that "none has promised it can produce machines at a cost that can compete with conventional models of instructions" (p. 121). No one seemed interested in the answers. The spirit of the times pointed elsewhere. Today, the spirit of the times argues that it is foolish to spend money on machines while paying teachers a fool's wage.

In the midst of the energy crises of the 1970s *Business Week* ran a cover story entitled "The Coming Boom in Solar Energy." According to the article the solar energy industry was about to grow tremendously as the federal government pumped billions of dollars into it. Then Secretary of Energy James Schlesinger noted that solar energy "may soon be the fastest growing part of our energy supply."[8] Some predictions held that solar would constitute 34 quadrillion Btu by the year 2000. In 1978 it contributed only 3 or 4 quadrillion Btus. Explosive growth was expected for both the industry and the markets it intended to serve.

There was only one problem. Some experts were worried that the solar industry was too small to absorb the massive amounts that were about to be spent on it. Not surprisingly, it turned out to be no problem at all. The industry, fortified by new entrants, managed to absorb as much money as was thrown its way.

In fact, the solar energy business largely transformed itself into the solar energy research business. Devices of unimaginable wonder and complexity were built to save the nation from the grasp of unfriendly foreign suppliers. Solar had caught the imagination of the American public. Desert "power towers" were superheated by sun-tracking heliostats. Windmills spun endlessly on California hilllsides, generating more in the way of tax credits for their owners than energy for a dependent nation. Research opportunities boomed. Self-supporting business opportunities remained untenable. Now, as then, solar research remains uncompetitive with traditional fuel supplies. In fact, the decline in energy prices in the 1980s exacerbated the trend toward economic parity. As the 1980s progressed, the merits of huge expenditures were questioned. The level of funding faded with the rise of the new decade. The boom in solar energy never came. The boom in solar energy research went bust a few years later.

Finally, there is marine mining. Since the early 1960s many have seen great potential in mining the ocean floors. However, in addition to economic and technical problems, the unresolved issue of ownership of this resource is being debated between the developed and developing countries of the world.

Actually, the debate is over. Third World countries have instituted a worldwide licensing procedure, with the profits to be shared. American firms threaten not to abide by the agreement but are reluctant to move forward. Lawsuits and other legal uncertainties might follow. Depressed mineral prices and surpluses on land have also helped to thwart this development.

8

Successful Forecasts

Not all forecasts failed. Some successfully foresaw events that produced vibrant growth markets. This chapter lists the reasons why successful forecasts succeeded under headings that describe the general category of the success.

The space allocated to the success versus failures roughly matches the proportions found in real markets: Seven chapters are allocated to failures, while only one chapter covers the successes.

The most stunning conclusion to be drawn from a review of successful forecasts is that there are so few of them. Only about 20 percent of the forecasts examined could be classified as successes. Clearly, the record on growth market forecasting is not enviable.

There have been successes. Mostly the successes have centered on a handful of innovations that went on to create huge growth markets. Generally, forecasters have anticipated the developments that led to the major growth markets of the past few decades. Forecasts for microprocessors, computers, VCRs, microwave ovens, and other significant innovative products have been repeatedly mentioned in the business press over the past two decades. Unfortunately, those forecasts have been buried in a large pile of failures. The problem is trying to separate the few successes from the large number of failures with which they lie.

One reason why the failures outnumber the successes is that large growth markets have been rare in comparison with the number predicted. Simply put, there have been far more predictions for growth markets than there have been growth markets.

The successful forecasts can be classified into two groups: demographic forecasts of cohorts, which almost always hit their mark, and product forecasts based on an innovation that met a cursory cost-benefit comparison. Consider each in turn.

Demographic Projections

Demographic forecasts that sought to predict birthrates and other events that had not yet occurred often proved mistaken. But, for obvious reasons, forecasts that sought to predict the future size of various age groups in the U.S. population—cohorts, in the parlance of demographers—have been remarkably accurate, even when they predicted events twenty years out. In fact, forecasts that predicted the age of groups already alive proved to be more accurate than any other type of long-range prediction.

For example, in 1960 *Business Week* analyzed census data and concluded: "During the next twenty years the number of Americans over 75 will increase to 9 million."[1] This forecast of the elderly segment of the population proved close to perfect. The 1980 Census counted 8.94 million persons over the age of seventy-five. In addition, the forecasters correctly recognized the implications of an aging voting populace on government expenditure patterns. Attempts to cut the entitlements received by the elderly have faced strong opposition from this large, politically powerful segment of the population.

In 1961 *Business Week* predicted that by 1970 the number of Americans in their "late teens" to "early twenties" would skyrocket. Based on a comparison of census figures from 1950 and 1960, it concluded: "This is the baby boom in full bloom."[2]

The magazine correctly anticipated that this huge bulge in the population would create opportunities for such industries as "clothing, cars and education," and threats for others. In sum, it predicted that "the soaring sixties will soar." For the next decade the economy did just that, and the baby boom proved to be a major force in the economy of the 1960s and beyond.

Five years later, in 1965, *Business Week* again looked at population growth and again correctly predicted the explosive growth of the under-twenty-five segment (up 58 percent), and the growth in the number of those over sixty-five (up 50 percent). It also noted that an increased emphasis on quality of life and a focus on rational family planning would reduce fertility rates and lower the size of families.[3]

Five years after that, in 1970, Census Director George H. Brown told a meeting of economists that by 1985—fifteen years into the future—the economy would be booming, incomes and purchasing power would be up, marriages would reach record levels, and the demand for housing would soar.[4] The reason was the tremendous growth in the 25–44-year-olds in the population. On almost all counts his fifteen-year forecasts were right on target.

The accuracy of those demographic forecasts is not surprising. Constructing such forecasts is largely a function of projecting younger cohorts. It is easy to predict with great certainty that a person, or group of persons, age ten will be twenty years old in exactly ten years.

It is also likely to remain an accurate type of forecast in the years ahead. Unlike forecasting in many other business applications, the process that drives aging is known and immutable. When you forecast age you are standing on firm ground. Consequently, forecasts that today call for huge numbers of elderly as the baby-boom generation ages should be believed. They are likely to prove correct, offering, once again, opportunities and problems for business and government alike.

Marketing Implications of Demographic Forecasts

The value of accurate age-group forecasts lies in the opportunities that can be gleaned from them. As noted above, it was obvious more than twenty-five years ago that as the postwar "baby boom" aged it would swell the ranks of various age groups. Given the near certainty of that trend, the question then became one of assessing the opportunities and problems the group would present as it progressed through life.

The horrendous errors presented in previous chapters often ignored, or ran counter to, those fundamental marketing factors.

Instead, they relied on far more uncertain criteria, such as extrapolating existing technological trends, even though those trends had no life of their own.

Attending to fundamental demographic changes has worked well in the past. Burton Malkiel, in his fine book *A Random Walk Down Wall Street*, tells the tale of how he made money in the stock market. In 1959 he noticed many young and attractive women walking on Wall Street. Census data confirmed that many more would follow. He asked himself what product those women would need. Whatever it was, there would be a great demand for it in the coming years. He followed his own advice and invested in a small company named Tampax, which had excellent distribution and weak competition. Tampax grew exponentially between 1959 and 1972 as young girls entered the market for its primary product. Both he and Tampax profited from their foresight. In his own words, "future earnings growth for Tampax seemed a pretty good bet in an uncertain world."[5] Demographics were at the root of that successful stock prediction.

Many growth markets have been helped by favorable demographic trends. Microwave ovens, for example, were first introduced right after World War II. But until the 1960s they were used almost exclusively in commercial applications outside the home. It was nearly twenty-five years before the product found its way into the home and grew rapidly. Interestingly, sales of microwaves grew at the same time as the number and percentage of working women increased. In large part, sales exploded because the primary benefit offered by the product—fast cooking—matched the needs of working women. The owner of a large appliance outlet noted: "We're getting a huge boost from working couples who have more money and less time to spend in the kitchen."[6] Like a newly discovered rock star, after twenty-five years on the market the product took off overnight.

The rapid diffusion of the microwave oven, twenty-five years after it had been introduced, created opportunities for some marketers and problems for others. Gourmet frozen foods grew rapidly, while Swanson's TV dinners, an innovation from another era—"space" food from the 1950s packaged in metal trays that could not be used in microwaves—looked dated on retailers' shelves. In fact, even the Campbell's Soup chief executive called the product "junk food." He observed that "it was great in 1950, but in today's world it didn't go in the microwave; it didn't represent variety or a good eating experience to my palate."[7] Demographics had changed the character of frozen foods. Lean cuisine and other gourmet products flourished, while TV dinners became obsolete.

Even political instability in Third World countries has been attributed to demographic trends. Marvin Cetron, a popular futurist, claims that potential revolutions in Third World countries can be spotted by looking at the percentage of young males in their late teens and twenties in the population—rabble-rousers of international renown. If there are many of them, watch out, trouble is likely. This cohort is often responsible for political upheaval. In the late 1970s Iran fitted this pattern perfectly, with catastrophic results for nonrevolutionary interests.

Cetron's observations are ominous, for many Third World countries—like Mexico—have huge percentages of their populations under the age of twenty. If he is right, many countries are in for many years of discontent.

Political trends in the United States have also been attributed to changing demographics. In 1978 one expert noted: "The growing mood of conservatism in American society is probably related to the maturation of the population and the waning of the youth culture."[8] The reason is fundamental. Clearly, the U.S. population is growing older. As the country grows older, there will be inexorable changes in consumption patterns and social attitudes. Consider the political changes that have come with this demographic change.

Contrast the political conservatism that began in the late 1970s with the rebellious, sometimes revolutionary, attitudes of the 1960s, when a much larger segment of the population was younger. From a demographic perspective such political changes should not be surprising, but from the perspective of someone projecting the political trends of the 1960s, the change is unpredictable. A prediction in the 1960s that within ten years the rebellious youth of the day would turn conservative, flood business schools in search of MBAs, and strive tirelessly for the almighty dollar would have been called anything but prescient. It is more likely that such a forecast would have been called crazy. It was clear during the 1960s that a new age, lubricated with drugs, had dawned, the Age of Aquarius. As often happens in forecasting, things were expected to continue on their present course, even though changes in fundamental factors suggested otherwise.

Economics are clearly affected by demographics. The same *Business Week* article noted: "Demographics make for dull reading but they helped lay the groundwork for our current economic problems." In the late 1970s it was apparent that the most rapidly increasing age group in the population was the 25–44-year-olds. By 1990, their numbers will swell by 35 percent, from 58 million in 1978 to 78 million. Historically, this cohort has exhibited the highest reading profile of all age groups in the U.S. population. As a result of those observations *Business Week* accurately predicted in 1978: "The 1980s, therefore, shapes up as a decade of enormous opportunities for growth as well as for severe strains on the economy. In the 1990s . . . growth will come harder" (p.66). The overall rate of unemployment, the magazine predicted, would begin to drop in the 1980s. Furthermore, it predicted that this group of consumers would continue to have fewer children than its parents, would have two-income households, and would stress quality products and convenience goods and services.

Those predictions turned out to be extremely accurate. The economy began an unprecedented recovery in early 1983 and has continued to grow into the late 1980s. Unemployment fell dramatically from the levels of the late 1970s. Also the younger consumers on whom this forecast focused do favor quality products, albeit mostly imported quality products, and patronize convenience goods at record levels.

Also in 1978, and before the decline in energy prices, a Rand Corporation demographer predicted that the aging population would slow down the migration from the Northeast and Midwest to the Sun Belt in the 1980s. He remarked that young adult groups are most likely to migrate. By the 1980s, he argued, migration would slow as that group aged, to be replaced by a smaller cohort. Whether by coincidence with the drop in energy prices or through a true reading of population dynamics, his prediction proved very accurate. The migration has slowed in step with the aging of the population.

In fact, one of the most amusing turnarounds in forecasting is the difference between forecasts of migration trends in the 1970s and the 1980s. Articles from the 1970s invariably told about the coming growth in such "new" and modern cities as Houston and the inevitable decline of older, seemingly obsolete cities such as New York. In 1972, for example, *Business Week* confidently predicted that the Sun Belt would continue to gain population from the North and Northeast. It stated, "By all accounts, this southward migration of people and business will continue through this decade and well into the 1980s."[9] The 1970s proved them right.

By the 1980s, however, the forecasts had changed. Now New York was touted as an international city with a diversified economic base, which was more immune to the whims of economic trends. Houston was excoriated as a single-industry town with unsolvable problems. Surely, other turns lie ahead. The financial crisis of October 1987, for example, is likely to hurt New York more than the rest of the country.

In 1967 *Advertising Age* reported that the population explosion would expand many markets.[10] Autos was one. Commerce Secretary Alexander Trowbridge told a conference of the American Advertising Federation that new car purchases could rise from 9.3 million in 1965 to 13 million in 1975. He missed by a mile. He focused on the overall size of the population, not on projecting cohorts. More important, the oil crisis of 1974 resulted in sales of only 6.7 million—barely more than half the predicted amount. He did, however, see that the labor force would grow rapidly as youngsters aged.

In 1966 Stephen Packer, writing in the *Financial Analysts Journal*, looked at how population growth would affect market forecasting. Specifically, he looked at how changes in the proportion of age groups in the U.S. population would affect sales of various product categories.

His study showed that automobile sales are affected more by economic factors than by the underlying demographics. Hence auto sales have not been affected by demographic trends alone.

Baby food sales, however, increased in step with the number of babies born during the 1950s and early 1960s and slowed with the decline in births in the 1963-64 period.

Beer sales, Packer concluded, are also strongly influenced by demographics. He noted that beer sales increased 14.2 percent between 1958 and 1964, along with a rapid growth in the number of 18–19-year-olds.

The robust growth of soft drinks was also influenced by the underlying demographics.

Parker's assessment of the value of demographics in market forecasting has held up over the more than twenty years since he conducted his study. He concludes:

> Population projects, made by applying sophisticated statistical techniques to historical patterns, can miss the market by substantial amounts over longer periods of time. Since forecasts of that portion of the population already born tend to be closer to the mark, projections of total population over shorter periods of time tend to be more accurate.[11]

After more than twenty years his advice is still sound, and often ignored. Forecasters still spend too much time and effort on elaborate forecasting techniques and not enough time on the fundamental factors that drive basic changes in markets.

Studies of the evolution of specific industries have also highlighted the forecasting power of demographics. Changes in those industries were influenced by foreseeable changes in underlying demographic factors.

Consumption of soft drinks grew rapidly in the 1950s and 1960s. Favorable demographics were a key factor in explaining the growth. Historically, heavy consumption has been concentrated among the younger age groups. As one analysis noted, "the U.S. has given a special blessing to producers of soft drinks: a bountiful supply of consumers between the ages of 13 and 24."[12] But in the late 1970s this supply of consumers began to shrink, and growth began to slow.

Beer sales followed a similar pattern. The growth in sales almost perfectly matched the growth in the number of younger consumers. In 1960, beer sales accelerated as the number of 18–34-year-olds soared—the group that accounts for more than 50 percent of consumption. Early on, it was clear to those in the industry that growth would slow when this demographic age passed out of the upper age limit of the heavy consumption group. In 1976, August A. Busch III stated: "The point is approaching, when our growth will be constrained by the industry's growth."[13] He was right and he was wrong. The 5 percent annual growth rate of the industry in the 1970s gave way to 3 percent growth in the 1980s. The reason: the aging of the primary market and the appeal of other beverages. On that point Busch was right. He was wrong in predicting that Anheuser-Busch's growth would be constrained by the industry's growth. Anheuser-Busch's growth proceeded at the expense of smaller brewers. Sometimes it is nice to be wrong.

Wine sales also benefited from favorable demographic trends. In the 1970s and early 1980s wine sales grew rapidly as the number of 25–54-year-olds grew. Furthermore, those consumers were well educated, had higher incomes than their parents, and lived mostly in large metropolitan areas. They were precisely the target market for wine. Sales were spectacular and grew rapidly for years. Growth slowed, however, with the aging of the target segment.

The growth of running shoes, housing, education, and a plethora of other products has been driven primarily by demographics. Slower growth for those products was also encountered when the demographics changed.

Assumptions of Demographic Forecasts

An important question for marketers and forecasters alike is whether younger cohorts will bring learned habits with them as they grow older, or will they adopt the products of their predecessors. As yet, the answer is unclear. There are strong arguments on both sides of the issue, and it is difficult to predict behavior in specific circumstances. Consider the following errors that have occurred in the past.

Forecasts are particularly vulnerable when they assume that a growth market will result when a large group of consumers enters the primary age for heavy demand of a product category. Such forecasts assume that the younger group will follow the pattern set by its parents. Often such assumptions prove mistaken. Groups of consumers frequently behave much differently from those who came before them.

Take the case of hats. Even a cursory look at old movies reveals that most men used to wear wide-brimmed hats. It was the style of the day. Entire cities, such as Danbury, Connecticut, were centers for the manufacture of hats. At one time Danbury was home to hundreds of hat makers. No more. The variety of hats has increased greatly, and many men wear no hats at all. Growth in the numbers of young men entering the work force did not portend growth for the hat industry. The industry declined with the trend toward hatless heads.

The market for scotch whisky also declined throughout the 1970s, even though at the time huge numbers of consumers entered the prime age of whisky consumption. The failure of light whisky is a classic in marketing.

A Balance Between Benefits and Price

At its most fundamental level, successful predictions of market growth succeed because forecasts are based on innovations that offer consumers a real or imagined benefit over the current way of doing things. In addition, that benefit must come at a price that consumers are willing to pay.

This is very soft language indeed, and it smacks of Monday morning quarterbacking. Sure, successful products offer a benefit at a fair price and unsuccessful products do not, a critic might conclude. It is easy to distinguish between the successes and failures after the fact. The unsuccessful products offer no benefit, while the successful products do. Is there really anything to be learned from this analysis? There is. Asking the right questions beforehand can often help tell the difference between the successes and the failures. Consider the following examples.

Place yourself back at the time the forecast was made. See if it is not often possible to separate the successes from the failures. Specifically, contrast the character of these innovations with those presented in previous chapters.

More than twenty years ago it was predicted that reflective glass would be widely used in office buildings of the future. In 1966 a sales manager for a firm advocating the product stated: "In five or 10 years, reflective glass will be commonplace."[14] It *has* become commonplace. As noted in the mid-1960s, it is aesthetically pleasing, energy-saving, and cost-effective. In short, it offered real economic advantages and the perceptual benefit of a clean, modern look. Furthermore, it did not cost appreciably more than existing building materials, and, once installed, it saved energy.

Contrast the case of reflective glass with forecasts for the widespread use of geodesic domes, underground buildings, and modular housing. Clearly, reflective glass is the least radical of those innovations. It does not require those who live or work in the structure to change their style of living or doing business. Geodesic domes, in contrast, are an extremely inefficient use of space, no matter how modern in concept. Decorating a geodesic dome is a difficult task: Vertical walls are nonexistent or must be created artificially with a great waste of space. Similarly, a corner office or bedroom in an underground building surely lacks the status of a corner office in a building made of reflective glass. Probably the only advantage those failed innovations had over reflective glass was that they were flashier, sexier, and far more radical. Unfortunately, they also proved to be far less practical. Their effect on the market was fleeting at best, misleading at worst.

The excitement of extreme forecasts seems to serve another master. Such forecasts jar the imagination more than those for more mundane innovations. Maybe we would all like to think that the future will be very different from the present. That way we might feel that we are really moving ahead.

Interestingly, in the early 1960s reflective glass began to penetrate the building market because it looked nice, not because of its cost. Only when sellers of the product stressed this benefit did sales accelerate.

All told, reflective glass was cost-effective, nice to look at, and compatible with traditional uses of business space. Even at the time, it should have been apparent which of the structural innovations was most likely to succeed.

In 1970 it was widely believed that electronic cash registers would inevitably replace mechanical models in retail establishments. Replacement costs were high, but the benefits were becoming indispensable. One industry analyst noted in 1970: "The primary justification for electronic cash registers is their potential for capturing point-of-sale information absolutely accurately and in a form that can be fed to computers at minimal cost." In this case, the benefits proved worth the costs. Consequently, predictions that "$1 billion worth of cash registers will be sold in the next 10 years" (by 1980) turned out to be largely correct.[15]

The product offered buyers a performance benefit over existing alternative product offerings, at a substantially lower price. Falling costs hastened the growth of the market. Other innovations, such as hydrogen fuel cells and photovoltaics, have not proved amenable to cost reductions. As a result, the market for these products has remained small even though they may have potential advantages (other than cost) over alternatives.

Facsimile machines lingered for decades until technological advances enhanced the benefits and allowed price declines to spawn a larger market. Only now, after many false starts, has the market for facsimile machines exploded. The balance between price and performance has been struck. The machines send documents faster and cheaper, and are now a "hot" product.

The growth of overnight package delivery followed a similar pattern. Federal Express was able to attract customers with faster service and lower prices. That was possible because of a process innovation based on consolidating shipments at a single centrally located base rather than relying on the historical industry standard of point-to-point service. An executive of the firm said in 1973, when the firm was only a little more than a year old, "We are about 10% below Air Express, and as much as 40% cheaper than freight forwarders." At the same time, an executive of Xerox, an earlier customer, declared: "Federal Express is the only freight outfit I deal with that consistently lives up to their commitments."[16] The combination of faster service and lower price resulted in tremendous successes for this firm. Again, those entrenched in allied industries failed to recognize the potential of this market.

Similar patterns were found in videocassette recorders, calculators, personal computers, and most products based on integrated circuits. Those products spawned huge growth markets that expanded rapidly as costs fell relative to the benefits they offered consumers.

Paper "cans," formally known as aseptic packaging, have been widely used to package fruit drinks, juices, and other food products. The reason is clear. This innovation offers clear benefits and lower costs as against metal cans. Paper cans eliminate bacteria and the accompanying need for refrigeration. They preserve vitamin content and cost significantly less than metal cans.[17]

Surprisingly, they have not replaced metal cans. Instead, they have created an entirely new market for single-serving juices.

The product is not new. It was originally developed in the United States in the 1920s but remained dormant until just after World War II, when Europeans adopted the technology. They reaped the biggest benefit from it. Refrigeration was scarce in Europe at the time. Currently, more than 80 percent of the world's milk is packaged in paper cans. Forecasting by analogy, and considering the cost-benefit position of the product in comparison to existing products, a bright future seems to lie ahead for paper cans.

Contrast the benefits of paper cans with dehydrated foods. Both innovations eliminate the need for refrigeration. But dehydrating foods negatively affects taste. Paper cans enhance food freshness without the use of preservatives. Dehydrated foods require consumers to change their food preferences. They change the texture of the food as well as the package. Paper cans change only the package.

Product benefits and disadvantages can be real or imagined. Contrast paper cans with irradiated foods, another packaging innovation. Irradiated foods have excited the interest of only those consumers concerned with eliminating nuclear energy from our lives. Irradiated foods are out of touch with the times, no matter what benefits their advocates claim for them.

Over the years, mixed in with predictions for 3-D television, ultrasonic dishwashers, commercial passenger rockets, and assorted other crazy ideas, have been numerous forecasts for video recorders and microwave ovens. Forecast after forecast has predicted a bright future for those two innovations. Each product was expected to create a huge growth market. Each did. Microwaves and video recorders turned out to be two of the most successful household innovations of the past few decades. Nearly 50 percent of American households now own one. But blockbusters of this magnitude are few and far between. Consequently, so are accurate forecasts that anticipate such stunning growth. Video cassette recorders and microwave ovens are the exceptions in growth market forecasting. Consider the foresight of the following forecasts and remember the failures of previous chapters.

In 1967 the *Wall Street Journal* predicted that videocassette recorders and microwave ovens would soon make their way into American households.[18] High prices were an early obstacle, but prices were expected to drop. They did. The forecasts missed only in their zeal to foresee the specific uses to which the products would be put and the form they would take. Combining the microwave with a freezer to facilitate one-step, pushbutton, computerized storage-to-cooking sounded more like the Jetsons of the 1960s than Joneses of the 1980s. Similarly, some experts predicted that video recorders would allow housewives to watch *King Lear*. Like early forecasts for cable TV, proponents of video recorders often foresaw the high arts when consumers ultimately preferred lowbrow entertainment.

In August 1967 *Fortune* offered a similar, but less optimistic, forecast for video recorders.[19] The mass market was a few years away but coming. A black-and-white video recorder then cost $1,000. A color recorder was not yet available. Instant movies, like the failed Polaroid product, was a closer possibility. The microwave oven would take more than five years but eventually would make it. It was about as likely to be successful as the home dry cleaner.

At the beginning of 1967 *Business Week* noticed the potential of a booming market for video recorders. The product would be widely used to train salesmen, make presentations, and serve other industrial applications. The consumer market would come later. Some experts believed that a VCR "will have to sell at about $400 to become the 'home instant movie'—and that is still several years away."[20] As anticipated in these and many other forecasts, prices fell and volume soared.

A review of past forecasts for video recorders and microwave ovens illustrates the length of time required for even the most successful innovations to diffuse through a mass market. It also refutes the argument that we live in times of ever faster change. Both products were introduced into commercial markets shortly after World War II. Both took more than twenty years to catch fire in a large market. The revolution was characterized more by a series of fits and starts than by a smooth unfolding pattern. The way in which they achieved success suggests something other than rapid technological change. Progress was slow, erratic, and never assured. And this applies to two of the most successful innovations of the past few decades! The record for less successful innovations is even less impressive.

The path to success for each of those products was paved with a mix of expected and unexpected events. First, it was widely known that to be successful it was necessary to get costs down. But as costs fell, other factors came into play. Microwave ovens looked as if they were going to take off in the late 1960s, when consumer advocates noted that the ovens leaked radiation when dropped from great heights. The media dropped the "great heights" part of the research, and consumers surmised that they would be purchasing a very dangerous product. Consumers decided to cook with heat for a few years longer. Similarly, the success of video recorders is usually attributed to Sony's entry with Betamax in the mid-1970s. But market entries went on for years with the video recorder. Various interpretations of the product were introduced onto the market throughout the 1960s and 1970s. A review of those entries clearly reveals that the road to success for the VCR was far more rocky than the forecasts implied. Even for successful innovations, which are exceptions to begin with, the timing of market success and the broad path the product will follow are often obscured from view.

Growth by Government Regulation

Some growth markets are pushed by legislation that essentially requires consumers to purchase a particular product.

Sales of car seats for children grew rapidly in the early 1980s. Two factors combined to boost sales. First, the postwar baby boom produced a large number of women who, in turn, produced the children. Second, in the late 1970s, beginning with Tennessee in 1978, states began to pass child restraint laws that fostered market growth. You either bought a seat or got a ticket.

Smoke alarms took off for the same reason. In the mid-1970s, when the government pushed them—hotels and apartment houses were forced to install the devices, and homeowners were strongly urged to install more than one—the market exploded. When the country was protected, sales slowed.

A Focus on Fundamental Market Factors

Most of the successful predictions of growth markets examined in this study stressed fundamental market factors rather than historical precedent in the industry or the glamour of the underlying technology. Consider the following examples.

In the 1970s cigarette brands targeted specifically toward women grew considerably. The more marketing-oriented producers, such as Philip Morris, correctly anticipated the growth in the number of young women approaching the prime smoking age, as well as the ramifications of the women's equality movement on their industry (e.g., "You've come a long way, baby"). The confluence of those social and demographic trends kept overall cigarette sales growing, even in the face of indisputable negative health warnings. Women could not be persuaded to smoke a small cigar, but they willingly took up cigarette smoking in large numbers.

A similar strategy proved successful for Heublein when it aggressively peddled vodka in the early 1950s, introduced prepared cocktails in 1961, and pushed tequila in 1966. Based on "one of the most exhaustive research programs in the industry"— a consumer study of 7,167 adults selected to conform to census data—it found that "55% of the sample expressed a dislike for hard liquors" and that this dislike was most prominent "in the growth group of drinkers: women, younger men, members of the upper and middle classes, managerial, professional, and white-collar workers."[21] Less insightful producers chose to follow the historical pattern in the industry, which pointed to a market that was clearly "dominated by blends and heavy-bodied bonded whiskeys." As a result, over the next two decades sales of whiskies and other heavy-bodied spirits declined precipitously, while sales of vodka, tequila, and prepared cocktails soared. Tequila and vodka sales grew rapidly for the next fifteen years, and only now, as this group of consumers is aging, are sales starting to slow. Similarly, in the 1980 annual unit sales of prepared cocktails were ten times what they were in 1960.

Since 1976 the market for bottled waters has sustained impressive growth rates. As early as 1970, many large firms (Coca-Cola, Borden, Nestlé) bought into the industry in the belief that this represented an emerging market opportunity. Their initial motivation was based on the steady deterioration of tap water and a trend toward "health consciousness." One industry expert commented: "I think people are beginning to differentiate between water you take a bath in and water you put in your stomach."[22] The confluence of trends in demographics, declining water quality, and an appreciation of the value of a healthful diet proved them right.

The market for running shoes offers another example. It expanded rapidly during the 1970s, spawned by trends toward fitness and health. Many of the established "sneaker" manufacturers, such as Keds and Converse, failed to recognize that their markets were changing. While the market for jogging shoes grew rapidly, they stood on the sidelines with a high-quality image and watched the market run by. By the time they realized their mistake, it was too late. An analysis of the prospects for Keds observed that "the company will almost certainly remain shut out of the athletic-shoe market."[23] To date, it has failed to garner a dominant position in the athletic shoe market.

The Special Case of Computers

Most growth market forecasts, especially those for technological products, are grossly optimistic. The only industry where such dazzling predictions have consistently come to fruition is computers. The technological advances in this industry and the expansion of the market have been nothing short of phenomenal. The computer industry is one of those rare instances where optimism in forecasting seems to have paid off. Even some of the most boastful predictions have come true. In other industries, such optimistic forecasts would have led to horrendous errors. In computers they came to pass.

Integrated circuits were widely expected to create wondrous products and stunning growth markets. Over the past few decades there have been numerous calls for integrated circuits. As early as 1962 many foresaw the potential of those devices. It was widely, and correctly, predicted that integrated circuits would follow the time-honored pattern of increasing sales volume and declining unit costs as the technology was transferred to larger markets. In 1962 John W. Mauchly, one of the innovators of early computer technology, predicted: "By the 1980s businessmen will be carrying personal computers around in their coat pockets."[24] Given the widespread use of portable and laptop computers, and the fact that at the time (1962) computers had not been widely diffused even to business, his prediction is amazingly accurate. It was not unusual, however. Throughout the 1960s there were equally glowing forecasts for computer gear.

Similarly, *Fortune* reported in 1962: "These exquisite artifacts [microprocessors] may alter the electronics industry, economically as well as technologically, as dramatically as did the transistor."[25] They did. Unlike other sectors of the economy, technological changes in computers were dramatic, even if they were largely expected to occur.

In 1968, in response to critics who saw the end of growth in the computer industry, Thomas J. Watson of IBM noted that "there doesn't seem to be any real limit to the growth of the computer industry."[26]

Finally, in 1973 Intel's Robert N. Noyce stated that "the potential applications [for microcomputers] are almost unlimited."[27]

The most fascinating aspect of those predictions is that in almost any other industry they would have turned out to be far too optimistic. Only in the computer industry did perpetual boasting turn out to be accurate forecasting, until the slowdown of the mid-1980s.

The tremendous successes in the computer industry illustrate an important point about growth market forecasting. Accurate forecasts are less dependent on the rate of change than on the consistency and direction of change. Change has been rampant in computers; but it has moved the industry consistently upward. Technological advances have reduced costs, improved performance, and, as a result, expanded the market. In few other industries have prices declined so rapidly, opening up larger and larger markets, for decades. Consequently, even the most optimistic predictions of market growth have been largely correct. In many slower growth industries, change has been slower but has served to whipsaw firms in the industry rather than push the market forward. In growth market forecasting, rapid change in one direction is preferable to smaller erratic changes.

Forecasting the Impossible

Finally, an attention to fundamental market factors may reveal environmental changes that are usually deemed unpredictable. For example, most discussions of the turbulent times of the 1970s point to the oil crisis of 1974 as an example of random events that cannot be foreseen. Yet a *Business Week* editorial foresaw the oil crisis about two years before the actual event. It stated that "the stage is being set for an energy crisis in the U.S. by the end of this decade. . . . In a time of international crisis, oil supplies could be cut off."[28] Earlier articles offer similar predictions. In this case, at least, there is evidence that it was not the event that was totally unpredictable, but that forecasts of it were not heeded, possibly because the event had no precedent. There had been a steady trend toward increasing energy use with no previous major disruptions of supply. The timing of the *Business Week* forecast was off somewhat, but they correctly pinpointed the factors that would precipitate it.

9

Some Conclusions About Growth Markets

In order better to predict the emergence of growth markets it is necessary to understand better the patterns by which they emerge. Analysis of a 1960 forecast for an innovation in large-scale learning, which turned out to be a horrendous error, illustrates many of the conclusions that can be drawn from a study of the patterns of technological diffusion.

In 1960 education, jet airplanes, and television were issues of keen interest. One expert thought it would be a good idea to adapt airplanes to education. The result was airborne educational television, which called for a DC-6 to circle Indiana at 23,000 feet and feed educational programs to schools in six Midwestern states. The concept offered many advantages over old-fashioned classroom teaching. The first advantage accrued to teachers. "Freed from arduous preparation of lectures, 'she' [the teacher] should be able to give more special attention to individual students."[1] Second, there was a historical precedent for the project. The idea grew out of "Stratovision," which used a similar scheme to broadcast the 1948 Republican National Convention and was a great success. Surely, it was believed, "Stratovision" would serve other markets. Most important, airborne educational television married two enticing technologies of the day—airplanes and television—and used them to serve a burgeoning market of eager young minds. That put the innovation squarely at the forefront of technological innovation at the beginning of the 1960s.

Even a cursory analysis of the innovation reveals why it failed. Clearly an overreliance on technology blinded the forecasters to the serious drawbacks inherent in their scheme. For one, the preparation of lectures, no matter how arduous a task, is not an unwanted consequence of education, it is the job of teachers. Second, the system seems to offer an advantage to no one else! It is hard to fathom who else benefits from watching teachers teach on television. It looks like technological innovation for the sake of technology.

It was also a cost-be-damned innovation. Given the sorry state of teacher salaries, was it really more efficient to employ such technological prowess to educate children? Were the expected economies of scale that great? Probably not.

The forecast is a dandy. It falls into just about every possible trap available for a growth market forecast. It overreacts to the prevailing technologies of the day, is held hostage by the Zeitgeist, and overvalues the predictive force of historical precedent.

More important, and the concern of the rest of this chapter, this forecast also illustrates a typical pattern in technological forecasts. It failed badly but, like many other forecasts looking far into the future, offered a glinmmer of insight into what actually happened.

Airborne educational television foresaw the immense potential of communications technology but failed to foresee the ultimate form it would take when transformed into a usable product. It envisioned circling aircraft when it would be satellite technology that would dominate worldwide communications. The market for communication satellites boomed, while planes continued to circle airports, causing frustration and anger for the passengers they carried.

The prediction also missed the main uses to which the technology would be put. Satellite technology was ultimately used to transmit television programs, not classroom lectures. Teachers still teach in front of the classroom. It is the quiz shows that get beamed across the country.

The forecast for airborne television also did not foresee what markets the technology would ultimately serve. It turned out to be a vehicle for mass entertainment, not just a means of educating students.

In short, this prediction foresees a different technology being put to a different use to serve a different market from what was ultimately realized. As such it is remarkably typical of technological forecasts. Consider each of these lessons, plus a few others in turn.

Invention Does Not Always Lead to Commercial Success

One of the biggest mistakes made in technological forecasting occurs when the forecaster automatically assumes that a particular technology will inevitably serve a larger market. It is important to remember that most forecasts fail because they are unable to meet the grandiose expectations set for them. They prove much too optimistic.

Much of the research and writing on innovation, diffusion models, growth curves, product life cycles, and technological forecasting mistakenly gives the impression that the development of a new technology inevitably leads to commercial success. They all presuppose a strong upward pattern of growth. They make no allowance for failures.

Du Pont's experience with Kevlar illustrates the optimistic bias inherent in those schemes. Du Pont scored big with Nylon and Dacron but found a meager market with Kevlar. In hindsight it seems that Nylon, not Kevlar, was the exception.

In 1987 the *Wall Street Journal* reviewed Du Pont's experience with this miracle fiber. Kevlar is a lightweight fiber that is five times stronger than steel. But, after twenty-five years, $700 million in capital outlays, $200 million in losses, and more time and money than the company had ever before put into a single product, Kevlar has found only fringe uses in widely scattered markets. As the *Journal* notes: "Du Pont's difficulties illustrate that technological breakthroughs don't guarantee financial triumphs."[2]

Du Pont did worse with Corfam, which turned out to be one of the greatest marketing flops in history. Apparently, finding another Nylon is not so easy.

Similarly, the popular argument that successful innovations are the result of the vision and persistence of entrepreneurs can also mask the limits of technological innovation and lead to overly optimistic forecasts. According to this argument, successful innovations can be had if we only let crazy innovators be crazy and allow them to follow their mission. Detailed studies of very successful innovations support that claim. Indeed, successful innovations do arise from advocates who possess vision and drive. You cannot quarrel with the results. But extrapolating from an examination of only past successful innovations to all developments leads to overly optimistic forecasts.

Not all advocates who are driven by a vision discover innovations that lead to growth markets. More often than not, crazy innovators produce crazy ideas. Persistence and vision alone do not ensure that the advocate has a good idea. For every success, there are myriad cases where advocates have been driven by a vision of an innovation that led nowhere. There was probably an advocate for the Branson ultrasonic sewing machine who pursued the project with vision, drive, and vigor. Unfortunately, the times squashed that innovation.

Studies that focus only on successful innovations promote this bias. A similar study of the characteristics of successful long distance runners would yield similarly misleading results. Say we wanted to discover the essential elements of marathon winners. If we studied the top hundred runners in the world, we might conclude that all successful marathoners are skinny. Our finding would be true but hopelessly incomplete. We could not conclude that weight loss leads inexorably to winning marathons. Marathon winners might well be skinny, but not all skinny persons are marathon winners. In fact, some persons might even be skinny as a result of illness rather than fitness. As with technological products, studies of only the successes can often lead to forecasting failures.

Innovation Comes from the Outside

Real market needs can be solved in myriad ways. The significant new products that will pervade our lives are likely to come from unexpected sources. Odd as it may seem, important innovations rarely come from firms that would seem the most likely sources. Firms that are currently dominant in a given industry seem to be the least foresightful. It is the industry outsider that seems the most perceptive.

Many firms have failed to capitalize on technological developments because they came from outside their specific industry. Surprisingly, firms holding a commanding share of their market are often among the last to foresee potential threats to their bread-and-butter products. As a result, market leaders often miss the opportunities that they themselves should have created.

The evidence supporting this proposition is overwhelming and is encountered in industry after industry, year after year. Many of the biggest growth markets of the past few decades have been discovered by upstarts or industry outsiders. Industry leaders have paid dearly for their lack of insight. Still, in most situations, market leaders have either ignored the threat or embraced forecasts of great opportunities in innovations that flopped badly. Consider the extreme case of calculators, adding machines, and slide rules.

In 1967 Keuffel & Esser, a leading manufacturer of slide rules, was commissioned to study the future. Its study produced many interesting findings, some of which came to fruition, but most of which did not. One of the things it failed to foresee was that within five years the company's product would be obsolete, the victim of a substitute product, the electronic calculator. It ceased production in the early 1970s. By the end of the decade an executive of the firm stated: "Now we sell about 200 of them a year, tops."[3] Most sales are now made as souvenirs of a bygone era.

The experience of Keuffel & Esser may be extreme, but it is not rare. Typically, market leaders are complacent about innovations that affect their served markets. As a result, they fail to foresee the technological developments that will change their markets forever. They turn a blind eye to new trends and focus intently on their current products. They do not perceive imminent threats to their markets as imminent or threatening. As a result, they leave themselves vulnerable to the attacks of new entrants, who seem far better able to foresee the direction of change in the industry than they are.

The largest manufacturers of electromechanical adding machines also had much to lose from the advent of calculators. Yet none of them foresaw the impact calculators would have on their businesses. And none of them pursued this natural extension of their business until it was too late. The practical microprocessor forever changed the face of the adding machine business.

Industry after industry has followed this disturbing pattern. Ballpoint pens were not introduced by the leading fountain pen manufacturers. Ballpoint pens came from the entrepreneurial Biro brothers of Hungary, who perfected the product in that hotbed of technological innovation, Argentina. Although the U.S. patent rights to their invention were acquired by Eversharp and Eberhard Faber, the first ballpoint was introduced by Milton Reynolds, an entrepreneur who saw the product on sale in Argentina and circumvented the Biro patent.

Years later, the biggest ballpoint pen manufacturers did not introduce disposable ballpoint pens. Disposables came from Marcel Bich, a French entrepreneur. Industry leaders have shown a remarkable inability to foresee the turns ahead.

Video games did not come from the leaders in the board game industry, such as Parker Brothers or Mattel, although those firms should have seen themselves as in the game business rather than the more narrowly defined board game business. Video games were introduced by Nolan Bushnell, a "work-in-the-garage" inventor. Bushnell managed to sell his creation—Atari—to Warner Communications before the demand for videogames crashed.

In the 1970s, three brothers from Brooklyn recognized the need for denim jeans that fitted women. With a mix of heavy advertising and a prestige image, they launched designer jeans. Levis did not challenge their entry. Instead, it pursued Levis tailored classics, a line of finely made upscale men's clothing, to which its brand name could not be transferred. Tailored classics failed while Jordache soared. Levis had failed to perceive the future course that its markets would take—even though it should have been the pioneer of designer jeans.

In the ice cream industry, leaders stuck with their current products while Häagen-Dazs walked away with the high-margin, premium-quality, growth end of the market. Again, the line extension should have been a natural for the leaders.

Disposable diapers came from Procter & Gamble, an industry outsider. In the 1950s, disposable diapers were produced by small firms such as Chux. The diapers were expensive and were used mostly in situations where convenience was valued, such as traveling. Most families relied on service operations, which cleaned dirty cloth diapers. Kendall was the industry leader. P&G tested its diapers throughout the late 1950s and entered the market with Pampers in the 1960s. Kendall did not react until 1969. Its brand failed quickly and found itself stuck in a declining industry.

Paperback books did not come from the top publishers, although the product was a natural extension of their lines. They were introduced by an entrepreneur who was helped by the leading publishers. Publishers saw little threat from the upstart and sold the reprint rights to hardcovers for small amounts.

The examples are endless. Overnight package delivery was not introduced by UPS, the airlines, or the principal freight forwarders. It was introduced by Fred Smith's Federal Express, an industry upstart. But, again, the innovation should have been pioneered by the leaders in the package delivery industry. Instead, the industry consensus seemed to be that consolidating packages in a single city was a foolish idea, and speed of delivery was not an important benefit.

Radial tires were not introduced by Goodyear, Firestone, Goodrich, or any other American market leader. They came from Michelin. Apparently, the smaller French tiremaker understood the American market better than domestic industry leaders.

Semiconductors did not come from the largest makers of vacuum tubes. They too came from outside the industry. Almost none of the leading tube manufacturers made the transition to semiconductors. They withered with the tubes they produced.

The list goes on and on. Tampons were not introduced by the biggest makers of sanitary napkins. Digital watches were ignored by the Swiss watchmakers. Rough-terrain or "city" bikes did not come from the leading bicycle manufacturers. Running shoes did not come from the sneaker giants. Light Beer was introduced not by Anheuser-Busch or Miller, but by Rheingold. Both diet and caffeine-free soda did not come from Coke and Pepsi. Finally, wine coolers were introduced by an entrepreneur, not by the big soda, wine, or spirit makers. In every instance, as well as in myriad others, market leaders were amazingly myopic in their perception of emerging markets in their own backyards.

In 1968 Vincent Marotta was a successful real estate developer who ran out of financing. After looking at various new ventures he settled on the coffee business. Specifically, he developed the first Mr. Coffee machine, which entered the market in 1972. Since then, it has held the number one spot.

The domninant makers of coffee percolators did not see the threat they faced. They reacted to Marotta's innovation slowly. In the eyes of many experts there was little chance this device would interest consumers. Marotta correctly foresaw that it offered consumers many benefits. It was faster, brewed tastier coffee, and did not cost the consumer much more for those benefits.

Each of these innovations came from outside the industry that had the most to lose. Remarkably, time and time again, in industry after industry, market opportunities have been more apparent to outsiders than to those with a dominant position in the industry.

Ultimate Uses Are Unforeseen

Often, no one knows what to do with an invention once it is made. The use to which it will ultimately be put is rarely apparent at the beginning.

Entrepreneurs test the market with myriad uses. Most fail. But someone, either by luck or through insight, hits on the best application. From that point on incremental changes in the product gradually change the uses to which it is put.

Take helicopters. As recently as the late 1950s their use was unclear. The first practical flying helicopter did not fly until 1948. The Army liked them. In fact, the Vietnam War a decade later turned out to be one of the largest uses ever made of the product. They have also served as a cost-effective means of passenger transport on short-haul flights, a use once believed ideal for VSTOL (vertical or short takeoff and landing) aircraft. Helicopters, like many other innovations, seeped into their current markets like water through the cracks of a leaky floor. The cracks were not planned.

The ultimate use to which a new technology is put is usually unforeseen by inventors. For example, Univac pioneered commercial computers, only to lose its early lead to IBM. In 1950 Univac's market research predicted that by the year 2000 there would be one thousand computers in use. Its initial forecasts called for sales of about a dozen large mainframes to the Census Bureau, Bell Laboratories, the Atomic Energy Commission, and similar large-scale users.

In fact, by 1984 more than a million computers were in use. The percentage error of the forecast was huge, as were the consequences of this error to Univac.

The forecast failed because it was based on the mistaken assumption that the market for computers was for advanced scientific purposes. Univac did not foresee the extensive, but mundane, business applications to which those wonderful machines were mostly put. IBM's success was due to its focus on business customers rather than scientists.

Returning to the case of Kevlar, we find a product still in search of profitable uses. So far, it has been tried in myriad applications, most of which have not panned out: the 8-pound Army blankets used to protect the tired soldiers who had to carry them; the heavy-duty Kevlar cables that snapped in use; Kevlar sails for ships that tore to pieces; and Kevlar boots for hunting dogs. Du Pont's marketing manager for the miracle fiber nicely sums up the problem of spotting the ultimate uses to which a product is put: "Kevlar was the answer, but we didn't know for what."[4]

From the perspective of the people who enjoy its benefits, air-conditioning does not really condition the air as much as it cools it. But initially air-conditioners were used for other purposes. Willis Haviland Carrier developed the first device to control the humidity in a Brooklyn printing plant. The paper the company printed on had a nasty habit of soaking up moisture on those oppressively humid summer days. In 1902, the first air-conditioner solved the problem.

The Ultimate Form of the Product Is Unforeseen

The form an innovation takes also changes as the market evolves. But, again, it often evolves in unexpected and unforeseen ways, often in a manner that is deleterious to those who initially foresaw the potential of the market. Consider the case of projection TV.

Large-screen projection television qualifies as a true growth market. Introduced in the mid-1970s, sales have been growing since its introduction and growing rapidly since the economic recovery of 1983. One of the pioneers of this product category is Kloss Video of Waltham, Massachusetts. Its flagship entry, the Novabeam Model 100, is a two-piece front-projection system. In 1987 Kloss held between 40 and 50 percent of the market for front-projection systems.

But the form of the product changed as the market grew. Systems that project from behind the screen have steadily stolen share from front-projection systems. Back-projection systems eliminate the need to have a box in the middle of the customer's room. In fact, Kloss's pioneering front-projection systems have become nearly obsolete. According to the Electronics Industry Association, 350,000 projection TVs (of both types) were sold in 1987. Astonishingly, no more than 15,000 units, or 5 percent of the market, are front-projection systems. A former Kloss executive observed: "It's a shrinking market."[5] The pioneer is in deep financial trouble. As the market for projection TVs grows rapidly, Kloss finds that it has 50 percent of nothing. The ultimate form of projection television was different from the one envisioned.

It would be nice to conclude that the story of Kloss is an isolated tale. It is not. Typically, as the market for a new technological product grows, the form of that product evolves, often in ways that could not be envisioned by the inventors.

William J. Abernathy and James M. Utterback speak of the emergence of a "dominant design."[6] They argue that in the early stages of market development firms stress product innovation, which spawns many competing entries. Eventually a dominant design emerges, which is adopted by most producers. Later in the life cycle of the product, changes are made mostly in the process by which the product is made. Those process improvements are designed to make the product function more efficiently, at lower cost.

The Ultimate Customers Will Change

As the product form itself changes, so does the primary customer base for the product. Microwave ovens and videocassette recorders followed a time-honored pattern. They were originally targeted to industrial, not consumer, markets. Often the high initial price tag for a product makes this pattern necessary. As the price drops, the product moves into consumer markets.

Another common pattern, especially in the 1950s and 1960s, was the transference of technology from military and space applications to industrial markets, and then, finally, to consumer markets. Although that is often put forward as a reason for funding the space program, the output of practical innovations has been meager compared with the expenditures.

One recent example of a space substance that made its way into consumer markets is Kangaroo running shoes. The transfer was made by an entrepreneur. It seems astronauts will need lightweight cushioned shoes when they stroll on distant planets. Fortunately, earthbound runners appreciate the same benefits. Kangaroo went to NASA, obtained permission to use the Dyna-coil substance, and made running shoes. It also obtained a delightful marketing hook for its product.

Kevlar was originally targeted to tire manufacturers. They were to use it instead of steel belts in radial tires. It did not work out as expected. The tiremakers decided to stick with steel, because it cost less, and it was widely believed that customers would respond more favorably to the manufacturer who sold steel-belted, as opposed to Kevlar-belted, radials. No matter how big a breakthrough the new fiber was, steel means strong in the minds of consumers. Kevlar was forced to satisfy the smaller market for race car tires. It was difficult to justify a $700 million plant for such a small market.

Growth Takes Longer Than Expected

Contrary to the often touted belief that the world is changing ever faster, a review of past innovations clearly shows that it takes a long time for an innovation to find commercial success. Like overnight sensations in the entertainment industry, many "new" technological products spend years perfecting their acts in seedy nightclubs on the unfashionable side of town.

Transistors, one of the most successful innovations of the twentieth century, were invented a little more than forty years ago at Bell Labs. It took nearly a decade before the devices were used in computers, and decades more before they made their way into consumer products.

The microwave oven, and the forecasts for it, for example, took more than twenty years to succeed. Developed right after World War II, the product served commercial and institutional markets, suffered from bad publicity about radiation leaks, and failed to excite consumer interest. Then, in the mid-1970s, sales accelerated.

Most other technological innovations followed the same pattern. TV, color TV, and numerous other successful inventions, from the turn of the century to current decades, took many years before they had a substantial impact on the markets they sought to serve. Many of those less than rapid penetrations run counter to the prevailing belief that markets are changing so much faster today. For most technological innovations, today, like yesterday, it still takes a long time to penetrate a large market with a major innovation.

Numerous studies support this basic finding. The Battelle Institute studied the issue and found that, on average, it took 19.2 years for an innovation to succeed.

John Jewkes, David Sawers, and Richard Stillerman, in a fantastic book published way back in 1959 entitled *The Sources of Invention*, came to similar conclusions. After studying myriad inventions they found that most took decades to progress from invention to a commercial product. They too questioned whether technological innovation was really moving faster in the modern age of the late 1950s. They question the "widespread faith that we are much cleverer and more energetic than our ancestors."[7] It is a great question that should be asked more frequently today.

Ralph Biggadike looked at the actual performance of new corporate ventures. He found "that new ventures need, on average, eight years before they reach profitability."[8] His findings make for difficult selling in a world of shortened time horizons.

Persistence and patience are essential in innovation. A forecast for an innovation is likely to succeed only if it recognizes that we are talking about long time frames.

Long time frames may apply equally to the time it takes until the product becomes a success and the time it takes until it fades from the market. Interestingly, a study of the top twenty-five brands of the 1920s shows that twenty-three of them are still number one in their product category.

Timing Is Crucial

Like that popular wine, no technological product can spawn a growth market before its time. Diet beer, bottled waters, microwave ovens, and even the building of the Panama Canal did not succeed until certain technological developments had been made and the market was receptive for those innovations.

The "ripeness" of a market is a key factor affecting the success of timing. While marketers may enable or hasten the growth of markets, the process by which markets emerge seems to be largely beyond their control. For example, microwave ovens languished on the market for many years until the trend toward smaller dual-income families created a market that valued the convenience the product offered. Many other growth markets have been spawned by the trend toward health consciousness that is so pervasive. Perrier's success is largely attributable to good market timing. Similarly, demand for diet soft drinks seemed to explode just as Diet-Rite entered the market. Weight-watching consumers of the early 1960s were discovering the merits of sugar-free soft drinks about the same time that Royal Crown recognized the potential of the market.

Derek Abell's notion of "Strategic Windows" speaks to a similar issue.[9] He contends that as the world moves forward, opportunities are created for some firms and taken away from others. He argues that firms should closely monitor the environment for strategic windows that are "opening." This strongly implies that markets are not created but identified. It also implies that markets are driven largely by outside forces.

Market timing for product entry, like market timing for stock trading, is a difficult, but critical, element in the innovation process. The immense success of Nike running shoes, for example, would never have been as big as it was had it not been for the fitness boom that began in the mid-1970s. Sellers of tobacco, alcoholic beverages, and other products for whom the strategic window is closing have a tougher task at hand. They are bicycling uphill and against the wind.

10

Improving the Accuracy
of Growth Market Forecasts

If you laughed loudly at the errors presented in previous chapters and were intrigued by the successes of the past, consider the lessons that can be learned from them. Clearly, the value of those forecasts lies in the lessons they provide. If nothing can be learned from them, then those examples serve solely to amuse and entertain.

Is it possible to learn anything from the outcome of past forecasts? Or are the outcomes unique and the lessons nonexistent? In previous chapters I have tried to show that there are consistent patterns among the forecasts, things that made the failures fail and the successes succeed. The patterns are useful to current forecasts. They are more than merely *post hoc* reasons attached to past forecasts with the benefit of perfect hindsight—so-called Monday morning quarterbacking.

On the following pages I argue that there is an opportunity for substantial improvement in growth market forecasting to be gained from a study of past errors and successes. The errors of the past can be avoided in the future by asking the right questions and attending to a few simple guidelines.

I offer three general guidelines, which, along with a number of specific actions, can improve on the historical record. These guidelines are simple and obvious—intentionally so. They are not shallow gloss-overs based on a superficial analysis. They are tools in tune with the job at hand. They closely match the fluid nature of growth market forecasting. Whereas mathematical models assume the precision of a chemistry experiment, these guidelines provide a way to approach forecasting problems. It is tough to nail Jell-O to the wall. It is no easier with a device powered by lasers. To believe that advanced techniques can lead to more accurate growth market forecasts is to deceive yourself. They just don't work in such applications. A forecaster who tells you otherwise is either lying or misinformed.

The guidelines provided in this chapter are also consistent with recent findings in other areas of forecasting: economic, political, production, and even weather forecasting. It is clear that complexity of analysis does not pay off when you are dealing with the future. When you are dealing with growth market forecasting, that goes double.

But, by using the guidelines presented in this chapter, you can expect to do better than forecasters have done in the past. Even cynics will be able to offer few alternatives for improving the record.

Still, it is important to state explicitly that no set of guidelines, or forecasting model, will ever guarantee success in growth market forecasting. Grandiose claims of much greater accuracy are just not warranted, and I do not make them. The very nature of the problem ensures that success can never be guaranteed. At best, these guidelines can improve the odds. The process by which growth markets emerge is inherently uncertain and will always be fraught with extreme risk.

Given that caveat, consider the following three guidelines and ponder their value. Together they offer the best opportunity to avoid the errors of the past.

Three General Guidelines

There are three general guidelines that can help avoid the errors of the past. Essentially they are a reiteration, and summary, of the central points made in the previous chapters. These guidelines are simple and obvious, but powerful. Surprisingly, they are often ignored. As a result, the errors of the past are repeated time and again. You can break that cycle by attending to these three guidelines when constructing or evaluating growth market forecasts. They offer the best opportunity for obtaining more accurate growth market forecasts, if only they are not forgotten.

Avoid Technological Wonder

The most obvious advice to be gleaned from a study of past forecasts is to avoid falling in love with the underlying technology. The most outlandish errors uncovered in this study failed for this reason. Many of those predictions were made at a time when there was euphoria in the air about a particular technology. Often it was believed that the new technology would transform our lives greatly. Consequently, the forecasts would call for great changes in the way we led our lives.

More often than not, the technology went on to serve a much smaller market, humbling the forecasters who saw fantastic visions. The failed forecasts proved fancifully dated and turned out to be grossly optimistic.

Often the cycle of euphoric expectations and mistaken forecasts repeats itself when a new technological development moves to the forefront, replacing the old technological development, which was new in its own day. Past mistakes are quickly forgotten to make room for the mistakes of the future.

The lesson here is not to be swayed by technological wonder. No matter how glorious the predictions for a new development or widespread the popular beliefs of the day, be forewarned and keep a keen sense of perspective. Do not be swept away by grand visions that call for great changes. In the past, the fever of excitement about most new technologies faded with time, along with the market potential for products based on it.

That may sound like ridiculously simple advice. It is. But it is advice that is routinely ignored. Avoiding technological wonder would have prevented more errors than any other guideline that can be offered. Think of the errors of the past before you evaluate today's forecasts. Keep those errors firmly planted at the front of your mind.

Consider recent forecasts for home shopping on TV and reading newspapers on a personal computer. Both have made little headway, because they are impractical. Videotex is another example. Does it serve any real need? Who is willing to pay for it? Over the very long term, those products may serve small markets. But they are unlikely to change our lives substantially. Forecasts for them are looking at the technology, not the market.

The advice I am offering is not to ignore technological forecasts, but to keep them in perspective and to recognize that they are most likely to prove much too optimistic. Pay attention to those forecasts, but remain skeptical. If you commit resources to them, do so on a very small scale and spread your risk among many projects. The real hits have been far fewer than the predicted hits.

Over the past three decades only a few technological developments—most notably computers and information processing—have lived up to the expectations held for them. There is no evidence that today's technological developments are any more potent that yesterday's

It is especially important to assess whether the forecasters are talking about technology or about the uses to which that technology can be put. If it is the technology that seems most important to the forecasters, watch out; you are being set up for a failure. It is the applications of the technology that move markets, not the technical aspects of the product. The most stunning failures of the past have been those that were enamored of the underlying technology to the exclusion of fundamental market factors. Discount growth market predictions that are in bed with the technology on which they are predicated.

Ask Fundamental Questions About Markets

Regardless of technological dazzle, true growth markets have been driven by fundamentals. Clearly, you should focus your attention on getting satisfactory answers to fundamental marketing questions.

Customers buy products for very basic reasons. It is amazing how often forecasters fail to ask fundamental questions about the markets they intend to serve. Do not make the same mistakes. Be sure to ask the following questions, which cover most of the basics:

Who are the customers?

How large is the market?

Will the proffered technology offer them a real benefit over existing and subsequent substitutes?

Is the technology cost-effective relative to those substitutes?
Is the derived benefit worth the price you will have to charge?
Are cost efficiencies probable?
Are social trends moving toward or away from this market?
Does the innovation require users to do things differently?
Does the innovation go against customs, culture, or established business practices?

Place the bulk of your effort into answering those questions. If you cannot obtain satisfactory answers, or if the forecasters seem more interested in other questions (especially technical issues about the product or the method used to forecast their diffusion)," revise your estimates downward. Conclude that the forecasters cannot tell you about the future demand for the product.

Be especially suspicious of forecasts made by forecasters enamored of statistical jargon. A good rule of thumb is to discount estimates in direct proportion to the number of times they mention "parameters," "estimation procedures," and "optimization techniques." Add similar jargon to your own rules of thumb.

People want to believe in magic bullets in forecasting. They do not exist. There is no forecasting method, no single approach to forecasting, that can do better than simply asking yourself these fundamental questions over and over again.

There are no seers with special information or statistical knowledge in growth market forecasting. Contrary to expectations, forecasts based on a long and complex analysis are no better than simpler forecasts. It just does not work that way in growth market forecasting. Anyone with normal abilities who asks the right questions can reach the limits of accuracy. Growth market forecasting, by its very nature, is an egalitarian exercise.

The best advice that derives from an examination of past forecasting errors is to focus on the practical uses to which a technology can be put. That is where the growth lies. Most forecasts fail not because they are based on innovations that proved technologically unfeasible but because the innovations fail to provide potential customers with something they want. Time and time again, proponents of a technological innovation mistakenly believe that the technology itself is what is important. Time and time again they are wrong. Most often, the success or failure of those innovations turned on the use to which they could be put.

Marketing questions are the most helpful. Ask yourself or, better yet, ask the forecasters who the initial market for the product is. Does it sound reasonable? What are the members of this market currently doing? What are they paying? Why should they switch?

Contrast the calculator with teleconferencing. The calculator did more of the same thing that adding machines did, except that they were lighter, had no moving parts, and were ultimately less expensive. They were sold to a large market of business and consumer users as a product substitute. Teleconferencing would also serve the business market (it was to serve the consumer market in its initial manifestation as the picture telephone). It was less expensive than physical travel, which it sought to replace. But it was unreasonable. Pressing the flesh and glancing around the table are integral parts of business transactions. Personal interactions will never be replaced by technological innovation for anything more than mundane repetitive transactions. Asking fundamental marketing questions would have enabled forecasters to gauge the market potential for those two innovations.

On the first page of this book I promised that studying past forecasts would permit you to tell why frozen foods made it while dehydrated and irradiated foods did not. Clearly, all three are technological advances. But asking simple marketing questions points up the problems with the two that have yet to make it in the market place. People do not want to live near nuclear plants. They certainly do not want to eat food with either a real or perceived connection to them. Dehydrated foods are also stuck in a small market. They do not taste as good as frozen foods. Whether they keep longer or taste better than they did in the past is unimportant to consumers.

Only a few of the forecasts examined here failed because they ran into technological problems. Electric car batteries that are competitive with the internal combusion engine, comparably efficient photovoltaic cells, and nuclear fusion are among the handful of innovations that have been held back primarily because of technological problems. Superconductivity, despite recent advances, is also a long way from providing a practical product.

Most of the forecasts that failed did so because they gravely misread the market they intended to serve. They saw trends where none existed. They were seduced by technical aspects of the project. They failed to ask the right questions.

The same advice applies today. Technological innovations will succeed or fail on the commercially viable uses to which they can be put. In the future, forecasts will continue to fail not because of technical problems but because the forecasters failed to ask fundamental marketing questions about the markets the innovations intend to serve. Asking the right questions is superior to finding elaborate answers to the wrong questions.

Stress Cost-Benefit Analysis

The most fundamental questions to ask of a growth market forecast is whether or not the product upon which it is based provides customers with something special and does so at a price that both the customer and the manufacturer will accept. As you will see, price performance comparisons are the linchpin of growth market forecasts. As you will also see, they are also notoriously difficult to predict. The relative standing of a new product vis-à-vis competitive offerings can change drastically as the market evolves.

ELIMINATE HAREBRAINED SCHEMES

The first and most clear-cut use of a simple price performance comparison is to screen out the most unlikely forecasts. Many growth market forecasts could have been eliminated immediately after such a simple test. It should have been clear at the very beginning that ridiculous products like undersea hotels and other fantastic and impractical visions in the past had almost no chance of spawning growth markets. Those innovations were no more than harebrained schemes. They failed to serve an intended market at any price. That should have signaled the forecasters that their forecasts were unlikely to come true.

It is not that the forecasters used the wrong method to conduct a cost-benefit analysis; they just ignored this essential ingredient altogether. While they were looking elsewhere, they were blindsided by economics.

Making a cursory assessment of price and performance is an easy, inexpensive, and remarkably effective means of discounting the value of forecasts based on uncompetitive innovations.

It is also more than merely Monday-morning quarterbacking. Scan the technological forecasts listed in the previous chapters and see if you do not agree that many of those schemes came nowhere close to being competitive. Artificial moons for lighting cities? Moving sidewalks? Preliminary cost-benefit scans add an often needed sense of perspective.

FORECASTING PRICE AND PERFORMANCE

Most technological forecasts are less clear-cut. The innovations upon which they are based are neither harebrained schemes nor sureshot winners. Initially, they might fail a price performance comparison. But, as the market evolves, they may or may not become competitive. These are the toughest cases. Changes in price and performance may occur but are not assured.

Successful forecasts are often predicated on innovations that initially have a high price, followed by declining costs and gains in performance. Most of the growth in computers, calculators, and information processing has been fostered by steady price declines.

During the past two decades much has been written about experience effects and a sister effect: economies of scale. Experience effects emphasize costs that decline over time as a firm produces a product longer and, in part, learns to do the job more effectively.

The opportunity for gaining experience effects can greatly affect the future price competitiveness of an innovation and the accuracy of a forecast based on it. Overall, the more likely and stronger the experience effects, the more likely an innovation will be to spawn a growth market.

But it is important to remember that cost declines are not automatic and should never be assumed. In many cases price declines are slow or nonexistent. They prove insufficient to make the product competitive. It is not as simple as merely calculating experience curves.

Some products never reach a competitive balance between price and performance. Some innovations remain stuck in an uncompetitive position. As a consequence, forecasts fall flat on their faces. Much of the market for solar-powered photovoltaic cells have not proved cost competitive with more traditional fuel sources. They have also been resistant to the dramatic cost declines necessary to penetrate large markets. Declines in fuel prices have worsened their competitive position.

Estimating future performance gains can be even more troublesome. Performance gains often come about through discoveries that cannot be predicted. As noted in the previous chapter, it is difficult to foresee the ultimate form an innovation will take.

Performance gains are also inextricably tied to prices. For years, prices of microwave ovens were too high to penetrate the consumer market. Demographics were important, but so were prices. Initially the market for microwaves was the food service industry. In 1965 *Business Week* noted: "At present, anyway, the microwave oven offers more benefits to the volume food handler than to the housewife."[1] Using microwaves to heat food from vending machines was an important market at the time. As prices fell the product moved into consumer markets.

Again, conservatism pays off in growth market forecasting. Initial projections should be for a small segment of the market where derived benefits can command higher prices. That skirts the issue of forecasting future price declines and sets a more reasonable target. It also allows for expansion from a position of strength.

It is especially important to direct your attention to the price performance characteristics of an innovation in comparison to competitive products. Although there is no mechanical procedure that can be used to calculate such comparisons, if you read enough of these cases you will learn what is important what is not. Contrast the cases of color TV and 3-D TV. Both were innovations of the 1960s. Both were widely hailed as likely developments. But only one made it. Using the guidelines presented in this section it should have been apparent why. The benefits of color TV are infinitely more practical thant 3-D TV. Color TV offered a substantial and valuable benefit over black-and-white TV. Three-dimensional TV offers an illusion that tantalizes for about fifteen minutes. Furthermore, it requires users to wear special glasses to achieve the illusion of three-dimensional action, a dubious benefit, which turned out to be no more than a gimmick.

VCRs and videodisks posed a similar comparison. It should have been obvious beforehand that VCRs would win out. VCRs offered consumers a coveted benefit: they could record programs off the air. That removed the stigma of complementary products.

Some products offer a cost advantage over existing products, but their benefit is questionable or requires that consumers rearrage their lives to use the product. Those innovations go against the prevailing customs, culture, or established, often embedded, practices of business and consumers alike. Innovations like food pills and teleconferencing argued lower costs. Both bombed because they were out of step with existing consumer practices.

The unpredictability of future price declines and future performance gains poses a dilemma for forecasters. While we know that a balance between price and performance is a linchpin for technological forecasts, it is difficult to know when, if ever, a balance will be struck between price and performance. We know only half of the story. We know that to be successful in the market place an innovation must offer an additional benefit to consumers at a price they are willing to pay. What we do not know is whether such a balance can be struck.

I have found that initial impressions, formed after a quick-and-dirty cost-benefit analysis, are the most predictive way of gauging the potential for consumer products. When I first hear of a major new product, I ask myself the fundamental questions listed above and conduct a preliminary price performance comparison vis-à-vis competitive products. I have learned that by listening further to the promoter's arguments, I will change my opinion—mostly from a pessimistic to an optimistic forecast—but in doing so, I decrease the accuracy of my forecast. Usually, when I change my mind, I change it from right to wrong. If I am not vigilant, the promoter will shift the argument to grandiose visions of technological wonder. Remember, focusing on competitive costs and benefits focuses attention on the essential elements of forecast accuracy. It minimizes the chance that attention will revert to technological factors. If you have read the forecasts reviewed in this book, along with the reasons why they failed or succeeded, your initial impressions will provide you with the best estimate of the forecast's likelihood.

With those three general admonitions firmly planted at the forefront of your mind, let's move on to some specific guidelines for improving the record of growth market forecasting.

Better Methods of Forecasting

Much of the work in forecasting has focused on forecasting methodology. I feel obliged to offer at least a little of the same. This section presents some specific methodological guidelines that can improve forecast accuracy. It is based on the historical record of past forecasts and the findings of other forecasters. The advice I offer is not controversial in the broader field of forecasting, although it might seem so on first reading. These guidelines take the form of approaches to embrace and actions to avoid.

No single powerful forecasting method is proposed. In fact, I advise you to stay away from anything that includes advanced mathematics. Simple rules are far more powerful in the fluid world of growth market forecasting. You must paint with a broad brush in such applications. Consider each stroke in turn.

Discount Extrapolations

Many technological forecasts fail because they assume incorrectly that the future will simply be an addition or subtraction from the present. Do not make the same mistake. Errors can occur in at least two ways. First, many forecasts simply add to or subtract from existing trends, assuming that the future will be a logical progression from the present. Second, and more insidious, forecasts extrapolate the issues of the day, on the mistaken assumption that the future will be driven by the issues that best describe the present.

BE SUSPICIOUS OF TREND PROJECTIONS

Many forecasts simply add to or subtract from existing trends. The projection that commercial passenger planes would continue to get faster and faster is an example of this type of projection. It led from prop planes to jets to the SST to the HST. But the trend broke after jets supplanted prop planes. The outrageous expense of very high-speed aircraft caused the industry to evolve in the way it did. As usual, trends proved subservient to fundamentals.

Take the trend toward larger TV screens that progressed

steadily throughout the 1950s and 1960s as another example. TV sets were growing steadily bigger. Then a second trend toward smaller screens emerged, pushed by the Japanese. As Americans made electronics disguised as furniture, the Japanese made portables. Unfortunately, the American firms, attracted by the higher margins of cabinet-based systems, continued to make those heavyweight systems even when the market moved away from them. The trend moved from smaller to larger sets, then switched to greater variability in set sizes.

There is an irony in those mistakes. While the forecasters were conservative in their orientation toward the market—they assumed that present trends would continue—they were often extravagant in their projection of it. They usually assumed that growth would accelerate. The opposite approach is preferable: Being creative in your orientation toward the market (defining the market and competition broadly) and conservative in your projection of it is a pattern that more often leads to success in growth market forecasting. In a nutshell, looking widely for smaller targets is more likely to promote success than looking intently for tremendous growth.

It is important to remember that a trend has no life of its own. A trend is the reflection of the underlying economics of the market. When the fundamental marketing factors shift, the trend moves with them. Focusing on trends alone is often a search for the will-o'-the-wisp.

Trends and patterns are quite capable of sudden and dramatic changes. Forecasts that rely on their continuation are often led in the wrong direction. While those forecasts glorify innovations that have no potential, real developments come from outside the industry. Tracing past trends and patterns is a poor way to forecast future growth markets.

Avoid Extrapolating the Issues of the Day

A second, and more insidious, error is the tendency to extrapolate the issues of the day, on the mistaken assumption that the future will be driven by the issues that describe the present. Predictions of continued extensive space travel, jet ships and jet autos, and nuclear devices of unimaginable wonder arose because they were dominant issues of their day.

The assumptions of a forecast are inexorably influenced by

the Zeitgeist, the spirit of the times. At a time when placing a man on the moon is of central importance, or lessening our dependence on imported oil is a national goal, the assumptions of forecasts were unduly colored by the issues of the day. Surely, it was assumed, those issues would continue to be dominant in the future.

Unfortunately, as the historical record of failed forecasts illustrates, the issues of one decade invariably give way to a different set of issues that dominate the next decade. There is a seemingly endless ebb and flow of issues as time progresses. In the past, at least, the "front-page" stories of one decade move to the back pages (or out of print) as the next decade emerges. There is no reason to expect that the future will change all that.

Ask yourself whether your forecast represents the popular thing to do or is something based on sound fundamentals. If you find yourself mimicking the popular lines of the day, beware. You may be pursuing an opportunity that will fade with the issues of the day.

Downplay Historical Precedent

Historical precedent often greatly colors growth market forecasts. Unfortunately, it is of limited value in predicting growth markets. What happened before in an industry often blinds those already in the industry to developments that come from outside. Often they assume that the roots of growth markets lie within their current experience. But, as we saw in the previous chapters, opportunities often come from outside an industry. There is often no historical precedent for the innovation in that industry. Consequently, industry leaders are caught napping.

Similarly, the fewer the number of innovations in the industry, the deeper industry leaders sleep. Stanford University's Nobel laureate Kenneth Arrow proposes an analogy known as the Earthquake Insurance Paradox, which can be applied to growth market forecasting. The paradox holds that as more years pass since the last big earthquake, people reduce their insurance coverage. But they should be doing exactly the opposite. The probability of an earthquake is increasing. By analogy, the pull of historical precedent becomes greater as past trends appear stronger. But often continued trends are indicative of coming bends.

Consider the Implications of Trends

Even when trends are spotted, the conclusions that forecasters draw from them can be mistaken. In fact, trends can mislead more often than they enlighten. Consider General Electric's experience with refrigerator redesign during the energy crisis of the 1970s. Planners believed that the confluence of two trends—costlier energy and smaller households—would lead to a growth market for smaller refrigerators. They failed to consider that small refrigerators looked out of place in existing kitchens and carried the negative connotation of self-imposed poverty with consumers. Rationally, consumers should have loved the product; in reality, they hated it.

That is a case where the implications of trends took precedent over fundamental marketing questions. Style, image, and the signals products send to friends and neighbors play a large part in whether consumers will purchase the product. The forecasters mistakenly favored trends over fundamental marketing questions.

Major markets often arise from unexpected sources with little respect for historical trends and precedent. They consistently violate the logic of rational planning. Consequently, the mechanical tools of science can often serve to mislead rather than to enlighten. Scientific analysis is of limited value in forecasting a fluid world. Those who possess a scientific bias often set themselves up for errors when seeking to discern growth market opportunities.

Strategic planning, as an ivory-tower discipline, has fallen on hard times for precisely those reasons. The logical flow of events it assumes often translates into costly mistakes rather than market opportunities.

Look Outside Your Industry

In growth market forecasting it is essential to attend to developments in other industries. In the past many innovations have come from the outside. Market leaders, while looking one way, were blindsided by these innovations, often never to recover.

Again, attending to developments in other industries can be a simple task. The important point is to cast a wide net in the hope of snaring many fish, rather than use a heavy hook and line to land a whopper. It might be as simple as regularly surveying the trade literature in a wide array of fields in search of potentially interesting developments. Making connections between widely dispersed fields can be far more fruitful than studying one area in excruciating detail. I am convinced that it is not the detail that counts in growth market forecasting. It is the broad strokes. A Renaissance man is more valuable than an expert in a narrow specialty.

If a project looks worthwhile, that is, if a potential growth market opportunity is discovered in another industry, it is advisable to pursue it. It is better to start small, however, than to jump in with both feet. This is covered in greater detail in the next chapter.

Most important, keep an open mind. Be aware of the historical record. Do not assume that your case is different. It is very possible that change will come from outside the industry, dealing you a deadly hand of instant obsolescence. A central part of any market forecasting operation should be to look regularly to developments in other industries.

DISTINGUISHING FADS FROM GROWTH MARKETS

Many market leaders have missed growth markets because they thought a technological development was only a fad. Many of those misses occurred because the new technology represented a break with historical trends. Consequently, market leaders saw no historical reason to focus on the threat until it was too late.

Consider the case of running shoes. In the 1970s running shoes replaced sneakers as the dominant form of recreational footwear. Nike pursued the new market vigorously. Keds, Converse, and a handful of other sneaker sellers seemed uninterested. A Converse executive later lamented: "We thought it would be a fad."[2] It was not.

Ironically, in the 1980s many consumers replaced their running shoes with aerobic shoes. Reebok, another newcomer, has succeeded handsomely at this change. Nike was not convinced.

Computers showed a similar cycle of newcomers foreseeing changes that market leaders felt would not occur, only to miss subsequent changes in their markets, foreseen by yet newer entrants. Digital built a solid position in minicomputers. IBM was late to pursue this product. Digital itself was less aggressive with personal computers. Those devices, it felt, would not supplant minis.

Similar experiences occurred in the soft drink and beer industry. When Royal Crown Cola introduced Diet Rite Cola in 1963, Coke and Pepsi did not respond. A change in consumption patterns was not expected any time soon. When Miller introduced Lite Beer in 1976, Anheuser-Busch did not react quickly. Previous attempts to enter the market with a "diet" beer by Rheingold in 1966 (with Gablingers) and Meister Brau (with Lite) were unsuccessful.

Trying to distinguish between fads and true growth markets is a treacherous task, but there are indicators. The speed of diffusion often says much about the longevity of diffusion. Markets that grow quickly, with a great deal of media hoopla, fall with equal rapidity. Consider the case of CB radios. During the energy crisis of the mid-1970s CB radios became a national craze. The lingo of cross-country truckers trying to evade the 55-mph speed limit was beatified by the media and consumers alike. In 1975 sales of CBs reached $400 million, three times what they were in 1974. It was only the beginning, the forecasts squawked in unison. By the 1980s everyone would go everywhere with a CB radio in hand. We would all be tied together. The market crashed when the big firms entered.

Fads seem to attract a great deal of attention all at once. They burn out as quickly as they grow. Consumers soon tire and move on to the next fad. True growth markets rise slowly.

Picking a Forecasting Method

There are many forecasting methods to choose from. They range from gut intuition to formal group consensus procedures to mathematical projections of past trends to projections based on analogous situations to highly complex econometric models. Researchers have built careers studying a single type of model. Generally their allegiances lie solely with this type of model, and their goals are to push forward the state of the art in that narrow niche.

The choice of a forecasting model for the types of problems examined here is not a crucial decision. At best, the choice is of secondary importance. Again, it is the broad brushes that matter in growth market forecasting, not the minutia modeled by a selected technique. Few of the forecasts that failed in previous chapters were in need of "fine tuning." They missed by a mile and would have missed by the same amount had they used a different methodology that relied on the same assumptions.

Consider the outcome of a 1969 forecast for vertical or short takeoff and landing aircraft, commonly referred to as VSTOL, constructed using something academics call a linear market share model. The model has the cachet of mathematics but fails for the same reasons as forecasts constructed using far less formal methods.

The VSTOL aircraft lift off like helicopters. The wings then pivot, and the craft flies like a conventional airplane. The trip from New York to Washington would take a mere thirty–eight minutes by VSTOL. Time would be saved because, unlike conventional aircraft, the VSTOL flies from downtown to downtown, eliminating the need for time-consuming taxi trips.

The mathematical market share model sought to discover how businessmen would travel between cities less than 400 miles apart in 1985. The model assumed four travel choices in 1985: (1) car, (2) conventional airplane, (3) helicopter, and (4) tiltwing VSTOL. It is all very formal and precise.

The model provided three predictions, all of which turned out to be mistaken. First, "V/STOL aircraft . . . landing downtown rather than in suburbia [would] capture 48% and 66% of the business travel."[3] It captured closer to zero percent. Second, the model predicted that tiltwing VSTOL aircraft would dominate helicopters by 1985. It never happened. So far only two tiltwings have been built, both for experimental rather than commercial aviation. Third, the model found that VSTOL would dominate conventional aircraft even though it was more expensive. It recognized that cost was unimportant to the business traveler, since he does not have to pay for the trip. But it failed to recognize that cost is very important to the airlines, the actual purchaser of the innovation. Airlines want to know how much VSTOL aircraft will cost and whether they will be safe. So far neither question has been answered to their satisfaction. The actual market shares of modes of intercity travel had little to do with the mathematics of the model and a lot to do with the assumptions it made about the airline industry. A fancier version of the same model would have fallen deeper into the same hole.

Unfortunately, the greatest effort in business forecasting has been spent on the development of new—and usually more complex—forecasting methodologies. Armies of researchers in myriad fields have spent millions of man-hours on methodological refinements. Most of the work has proceeded on the implicit assumption that methodological advances lead to more accurate forecasts.

In the past decade some researchers have shifted their efforts to comparing the actual forecasting performances of proposed forecasting methods. The results have surprised some and disturbed many others.

The overwhelming conclusion of recent research is that methodological enhancements do not provide forecasts that are any more accurate than simpler traditional approaches. That applies to not only the thorny problems of growth market forecasting but also to many other types of forecasting problems.

Nigel Calder, the famous futurist, seems to agree. He opts for simple qualitative methods of forecasting. He recommends what he calls sentence-making, where you simply sit down and say what and why. He argues that such an approach makes it much easier to recognize the garbage, since it is not dressed up in fancy methodology. It makes sense to me.

Neustadt and May in their excellent book *Thinking in Time* argue for the use of analogous situations, an innovative approach that relies on a reading of history.[4] They propose a series of simple, judgmental methods. I strongly recommend their book for those interested in growth market forecasting. Their method is well suited to ill-defined areas like growth market forecasting.

Analogous situations have a long history of use in growth market forecasting, although little formal work has been conducted on their value. Analogies across countries are common: the success of failure of a product in one country as a forecast for its success or failure in another. For example, sales of Digital Audio Tapes (DATs) in Japan have been disappointing despite inital claims that the product would supplant cassette tapes in the United States. Most forecasts have been revised downward in view of the lack of success in Japan.

Forecasting one product with an analogous one is also used.

Sales of color TV, for example, followed a similar pattern to sales of black-and-white TV more than a decade earlier. A carefully chosen product can serve as a helpful analogy.

Analogies are useful but, like trends, must be subservient to the general guidelines to avoid technological wonder, ask fundamental questions, and stress cost-benefit analysis, presented above. In my opinion, analogies are naturally more subservient to those guidelines than trends. Trends, to many, take on a life of their own.

Contrast the jet–SST–HST example presented earlier with the black–and–white and color TV example. The fundamentals for the TV example are solid. The jet–SST–HST example lacks all but a trend. This is not mere Monday-morning quarterbacking. The signals were there ahead of time. There was no good economic reason to develop the SST, and there is now no good reason to develop the HST. It is my belief that the trends will bend when government leaders perform a simple cost-benefit analysis.

The path to improving the record of growth market forecasting is not paved with complex analysis, it is paved with multiple methods. In fact, studying an issue in excruciating detail is more likely to hurt than to help. This is not an endorsement for a superficial analysis. Instead, it is an argument for looking at an issue from many different angles. Multiple methods are better than a single method when it comes to growth market forecasting.

If you are trying to predict or evaluate the potential of a growth market, try to use multiple methods. Ask questions, search for analogies, study the fundamentals, and compare the product with existing alternatives. Your confidence in the forecast should be proportional to the number of indicators that point in the same direction.

The support for multiple methods is plentiful. One of the most prominent findings of the forecasting literature is that multiple methods, combinations of forecasts, and averages of estimates are superior to forecasts based on only a single method. When given the choice, breadth of analysis almost always wins over depth of study. Multiple methods almost universally yield more accurate forecasts than a single forecasting model, no matter how elegant that model may be. This finding has held true for all types of forecasting. It is especially true for growth market forecasting, where data are scarce and judgment and intuition play central roles.

The argument for multiple methods is also an argument for finding satisfactory answers to the right questions, rather than elegant answers to the wrong questions.

Challenge Assumptions

The most important advice for improving the accuracy of growth market forecasts is to challenge the assumptions that underlie the forecasts. It is the underlying assumptions that are of crucial importance. If the assumptions are faulty, the forecast will be mistaken.

Consider the failures in previous chapters. They failed because they assumed something about the future that they should not have. The method did not matter, the assumptions did.

Fancy and elegant forecasting models are no less free of assumptions that less structured, intuitive-based methods of forecasting; their assumptions are simply better hidden. As the forecasts examined in this book illustrate, a forecast predicated on mistaken assumptions is more likely to fail than a forecast generated using a less than perfect method.

Simple models may in fact work best, because they assume the least. Any theoretical gain in forecast accuracy obtained from the use of a complex method is likely to be "beaten down" by the workings of the messy world in which we live.

William Ascher studied numerous past forecasts and found that those that failed did so because they were predicated on mistaken assumptions.[5] The model selected to generate the forecast was found to be of secondary importance at most. It is especially important to ask: How dependent are you on the dominant themes of the day? Many errant expectations have failed on this point. The "jet age" of the early 1960s, the "space age" of the mid-to-later 1960s, and the energy crisis of the 1970s all gave way to new dominant themes in subsequent periods. When those issues ebbed, so did many of the growth markets they were supposed to have spawned.

11

Strategic Alternatives
to Forecasting

The guidelines presented in the previous chapter can help avoid the horrendous errors of the past, but they cannot guarantee success. There are no magic bullets in growth market forecasting. To say that there is is to lie or to deceive yourself. Trying to discern something that, by definition, has not yet occurred is a treacherous task that often foils even the most reasoned efforts.

This chapter looks at the next best thing. It examines alternatives to forecasting. It argues that if forecasts themselves are highly unreliable, then maybe it is possible to sidestep the necessity to generate accurate market forecasts by adopting strategies that shift the problem elsewhere. The following approaches can help accomplish this task.

Scenario Analysis

Scenario analysis does not pretend to predict the future. Instead, it postulates a set of plausible futures, each of which is possible but not assured. Writing a set of scenarios helps to spread the risk by ensuring that a firm is not expecting something that it cannot possibly hope to know. It is an alternative to forecasting that is better suited to the uncertainties inherent in predicting the emergence of future growth markets.

Scenario analysis is not new, it is only newly rediscovered.

Herman Kahn originally popularized the technique in the 1950s, when he worked at the Rand Corporation. Since that time, most studies have focused on—you guessed it—methodological issues. There are many methods for constructing scenarios. What we do not know is whether any of them are worthwhile.

Many articles have been written on cross-impact analysis—a family of exotic mathematical models that seeks to quantify and manipulate the judgmental estimates of experts. The procedure exemplifies the madness of models over substance. Many researchers have focused on the mathematics of the technique and forgotten that the real purpose of their efforts is to generate better forecasts. Avoid this methodological wonder and any others like it that rely on elaborate schemes that shift the emphasis from the problem at hand to computer analysis.

What Makes Scenarios Different

The term "scenarios," like the technique itself, is ill-defined. Generally, when writers refer to scenarios they mean something that contains some combination of the following three characteristics.

FLOWING NARRATIVES

Scenarios are structured as flowing narratives. They are constructed as "prose" rather than numerical estimates. You write scenarios, whereas you calculate forecasts. Scenarios rely on insight, vision, and creativity. This bias toward the subjective highlights the vagaries of the future and stands in stark contrast to quantitative forecasts, which are usually presented with the false precision of four significant decimal places.

MULTIPLE SCENARIOS

Usually, more than one scenario is constructed. Each scenario describes a possible path to the future, and the entire set offers a plausible range of possibilities. The objective of multiple scenarios is to identify a set of possible futures instead of seeking to nail down that one elusive outcome that will ultimately be realized.

TRACES OF THE FLOW OF EVENTS

Scenarios frequently trace the progression of the present to the future rather than simply provide an estimate for some future period. They often indicate how you will get there, not just what it will look like when you arrive. That supposedly provides the user with insights into how change will occur rather than a mere point-estimate forecast.

Not everyone incorporates all three aspects into scenarios. Some adopt the narrative format but offer only a single forecast. Others offer multiple forecasts based on differing assumptions, but do not present the results in the form of a stylized narrative. Still others stress the "flow" of the present into the future but provide only a single scenario. In all cases, the results of their efforts are referred to as scenarios.

Strategies for Multiple Scenarios

The strength of scenarios lies in the strategies that can be derived from them. Unlike planning in expectation of a single forecast, multiple scenarios stress planning in expectation of many outcomes, each of which is possible, but none of which can be precisely identified beforehand. Three strategies are possible. What follows is a brief description of each.

Robust Strategies

If a firm cannot hope to ascertain which future it will face, it can develop a strategy that is resilient no matter which of many outcomes occurs. A robust strategy is designed to perform well over more than one outcome, irrespective of which is later realized. For example, if the cost declines of a technological innovation are uncertain, or if competing technological solutions exist, a robust strategy might be selected to minimize the damage done by each possible outcome. In that way the firm is least likely to be hurt badly if the unexpected occurs, which it often does. This strategy is a conservative response to an environment that is inherently unpredictable.

A robust strategy is similar in concept to hedging in investments. hedging takes positions on both sides of possible price movements. While hedging precludes enormous profits, it insures against large losses and provides stable, if more modest, gains. Investment strategies have embraced this notion; business strategies for entering growth markets with new technological products have generally relied on a single forecast, either implied or explicit.

A robust strategy accomplishes another task. It highlights the assumptions underlying a forecast, allowing them to be challenged vigorously. In designing such a strategy, managers are encouraged to conceive potential outcomes that might invalidate what is proposed. A strategy that proves robust to those challenges stands a better chance of success in an uncertain environment than one that is predicated on a host of hidden assumptions that often prove unfounded.

Consider the following case. Between 1979 and 1983 Goodrich invested $700 million in facilities to produce polyvinyl chloride (PVC). At the time it was widely believed that the main feedstocks for PVC would soon be in short supply. Goodrich thought it had spotted a vigorously growing market. It had not. Instead of robust growth, the decline in energy prices and severe overcapacity in the industry turned its investment into a disaster. In the mid-1980s it was trying to sell its facilities for a fraction of their original cost. Goodrich Chairman John D. Ong confessed, "We were dead wrong on our assumption."[1] A more vigorous challenge to the underlying assumptions might have pointed up the vulnerability of the forecasts and allowed the firm to hedge its bets.

A key advantage of a robust strategy is that it takes the emphasis off the development of accurate forecasts and places it squarely on the uncertainty of future outcomes. It proceeds on the proposition that a firm will face an unforeseeable future rather than one that can be identified precisely.

A robust strategy also ensures that the firm's strategy will not be invalidated even if the most likely future never occurs.

A robust strategy is not without drawbacks. By definition, it is risk-averse and is unlikely to prove optimal for any outcome. A robust strategy is willing to trade off the possibility for spectacular profts or market position for the assurance that some rewards will be realized.

Furthermore, hedging is not always possible. A survey by Harold Klein and Robert Linneman found that "straddle decisions," wherein a firm draws a plan that is "robust" to, or "straddles," multiple scenarios, are impossible in many capital-intensive industries.[2] In such instances, the decision is to proceed or not. There is no middle ground.

Flexible Strategies

Another strategy for dealing with an uncertain future is to remain flexible until the future becomes clearer. A flexible strategy keeps options open for as long as possible. It postpones commitment until the last possible moment. Then, a quick move is made.

This use of multiple scenarios incorporates two key components: flexibility and a quick move. The firm should strive to stay as flexible as possible so that it can move quickly in response to unexpected changes in the environment.

Many of the aspects of an innovation are unknown when it is new to the market. It is unclear how large the market for the product is. The ultimate uses to which it will be put are unknown. So is the ultimate form the product will take. Even the largest customer base often turns out to be far different than that envisioned. Maintaining flexibility—the ability to move to different product forms that serve different customers in different ways—is essential in an emerging market. Recognizing the changes quickly and moving with them are equally important. Ideally, multiple scenarios will convey the likelihood of each possibility.

Contingency planning is an example of a flexible strategy. The course of action is contingent upon events that have yet to occur. It is characterized by fluidity and an ability to change with the prevailing winds. One planner noted in the highly uncertain times following the 1974 oil embargo: "If you can't forecast all you can do is react quickly."[3] When uncertainty is high and forecasts can be expected to perform poorly, this may be the superior alternative.

A flexible strategy is formally implemented in two ways. First, *a separate strategy, or course of action, is constructed for each scenario.* Depending on which events occur, different strategies are put in place. A less formal response is also possible.

Second, it *stresses vigilance.* An integral part of a flexible strategy is an emphasis on spotting an outcome as soon as possible. It is a strategy based on the principal of fast reaction rather than long-range anticipation. An executive at Dow Chemical noted that plans "are too inflexible. We stress fast response time."[4] In a business environment characterized by poor forecasts of emerging markets, this strategy can have great appeal.

Often a firm constructs plans in expectation of the most probable scenario, with contingencies for possible divergences. In the mid-1980s ARCO faced a clouded future in regard to oil prices. After poring over hundreds of "what if" scenarios, it concluded that the "disaster scenarios" of falling oil prices was a real, but uncertain, possibility. In response, it reduced spending on exploration and production, closed downstream businesses, and shut marginal chemical operations. However, it also prepared against the prospect of rising oil prices by focusing testing on a massive Alaskan field.[5] It was keeping its options open, ready to move quickly if events changed the outlook for its business.

Another manifestation of a flexible strategy is to spend heavily on R&D but postpone product introduction until a competitor has reduced uncertainty. In the case of pioneering a radically new product, that means letting competitors enter first, proving the potential of the market, before entering with an improved product. IBM appears to follow this strategy consistently. It consistently ranks as one of the heaviest spenders on R&D but is generally not the first to introduce important innovations. Instead, it postpones entry until the innovation's potential has been proved, then enters with a product that unfailingly earns it a dominant position. More on this strategy for avoiding growth market forecasts is presented later in this chapter.

The primary benefit of a flexible strategy accrues from the passage of time. By waiting until the flow of events becomes clearer, a firm can move later, but more intelligently, toward a growth market opportunity. Likewise, it can avoid being burned badly by market opportunities that never materialize.

Multiple Coverage Strategies

Another alternative to forecasting growth markets is to pursue many projects simultaneously. For example, throughout the late 1960s and the 1970s, RCA pursued both videodisks and video-cassette recorders because it was unsure which technology would dominate. The videodisk system failed, but it was the first American company to enter the market with a VHS format VCR (made by Matsushita) in response to Sony's Betamax.

For firms with the resources for it, a multiple coverage strategy is an ideal way to insure against missed opportunities. By pursuing alternatives, the firm minimizes the risks of the entrepreneur but increases the odds of reaping his rewards.

A multiple coverage strategy is also beneficial to firms that serve large segmented markets and are threatened on multiple fronts. Multiple options allow them to maintain a dominant position in such markets. It is an alternative to the "niche" strategy available to firms with fewer resources.

The primary drawback of this strategy is its expense. Resources must be allocated over a wider array of options. Consequently, it is available only to well-heeled competitors with the resources to allocate. Smaller firms would have to spread their resources too thin to employ this strategy effectively.

How to Avoid Focusing on a Single Scenario

The least desirable way of dealing with multiple scenarios is to focus on a single scenario and ignore others in the set. This negates the central premise of the method and defaults to planning against a single future.

Apparently there is an irresistible urge to focus on a single scenario. It must be physiological, originating in the same part of the brain as sex and hunger. Attempts to get users to consider the entire set has focused on varying the number of scenarios presented to users, changing the manner in which they are arrayed, and deciding whether to attach probabilities to each scenario.

The problem is that while people have spoken extensively on those issues, they often disagree. More troubling, there have been surprisingly few empirical studies on the merits of multiple scenarios. Still, three simple preliminary guidelines can be offered to minimize the temptation to focus on a single scenario. In the absence of strong evidence to the contrary, they are the best rules to follow. Each is described below.

AVOID PROBABILITIES

The evidence is clear on this point: Do not attach probabilities to multiple scenarios. It conveys the sense of a precision that simply does not exist. Instead, try to construct scenarios that appear equally likely. It better captures the underlying uncertainty and forces users to consider each scenario as plausible.

ESTABLISH CLEAR THEMES

Constructing clear and independent themes seems to be the better choice. For example, instead of assigning the probabilities of 50, 30, and 20 percent to a set of three scenarios, array them with clear descriptive themes such as "rapid experience effects," "slow market acceptance," and "the emergence of a competing technological solution." Each theme captures a key attribute of the possible future. It also helps to coalesce the central points when writing each scenario.

This scheme is also superior to arraying scenarios according to the popular "optimistic," "pessimistic," and "middle ground" criteria. It is more likely that users will focus on the "middle ground" scenario and ignore the other two.

Martin Topol and I ran some experiments using the optimistic/pessimistic/middle ground scheme. We found that users favored the scenarios that best fitted their preconceived notions about which event was most likely and ignored the others. We also found that their preconceived notions did not improve the accuracy of year-to-year sales forecasts.[6]

Other schemes also favor a single scenario. Labeling one scenario "most likely" and bracketing it with two "bounding" scenarios creates a tendency for a user to favor the "most likely" scenario and to discount the others as unlikely to occur.

USE TWO, THREE, OR FOUR SCENARIOS

Two to four scenarios is probably the best number to choose. Within that range it probably makes little difference how many are used. Selections should be made using other criteria, such as how many seem appropriate for the application at hand.

In sum, scenarios are not a holy grail. They are an alternative course of action in situations where forecasts are of suspect accuracy. In such situations, the advantages of scenarios exceed those of traditional models. Surely, scenarios are superior to a strategy of developing ever more elegant forecasting models, whose predictions turn out to be as mistaken as the assumptions on which they are based.

Follow Rather Than Lead

Another alternative to poor forecasts is a variation of the flexibility strategy presented above. This altenative has a simple but controversial premise. It argues that it is better to wait until the potential of a new technological product becomes apparent, then enter the market after someone else has pioneered it, than it is to attempt to forecast which technologies will result in successful products and which will not. It is a strategy that avoids innovation and seems downright un-American. But it has been widely used and has worked very well in the past, especially for large firms with the resources to muscle their way into the action. Later entry works especially well when a firm possesses some special competence, such as guaranteed distribution or advertising muscle, that it can use to counteract the vision of more insightful, but less well endowed, competitors.

Over the years, a proactive policy of innovation has been the preferred path to market dominance. This policy assumes that pioneers will gain a large share of a growing market and will be able to hang on to it.

According to experts, firms that enter the market later are forced to imitate the moves of more insightful competitors. Implicit in that dictum is the belief that imitators should be embarrassed by their lack of insight. It is also believed that they will pay a heavy price and will never be able to make up for lost time.

The reasons why pioneering firms succeed are many:

- Consumers know and favor the pioneer's product. They have no reason to experiment with subsequent entries.
- Experience effects accrue more quickly to the pioneer than to later entrants, placing later entrants at a competitive cost disadvantage.
- Pioneers can erect entry barriers that lock out subsequent entrants.

Ted Levitt, in an article entitled "Exploit the Product Life Cycle," published in the *Harvard Business Review,* is one of the few to come out in favor of later entry. In 1965 he observed humorously: "The trouble with being a pioneer is that the pioneers get killed by the Indians."[7] One year later, in an article entitled "Innovative Imitation," he recognized that opposing innovation was akin to opposing motherhood or apple pie but added that "imitation is not only more abundant than innovation, but actually a much more prevalent road to business growth and profits."[8] Apparently, a strategy predicated on reverse engineering and an ability to respond quickly to innovations introduced by competitors can work well.

A look back at the actions of past competitors shows that many firms with a strong marketing orientation embrace later entry. Procter & Gamble has relied heavily on later entry to dominate markets pioneered by others. So has IBM. Similarly, Coca-Cola's entry strategy was summed up by one of its marketing managers in this way: "We let others come out, stand back and watch, and then see what it takes to take the category over."[9]

A review of the historical record also indicates that later entry is often successful. Often pioneers do not retain their dominant position. Instead, they provide a test market for subsequent entrants, who learn from their mistakes and improve on their performance. Merle Crawford, in his comprehensive text on new product management, writes that "a product entering the market is merely a version of an idea. The product will soon change again in response to the marketplace."[10] Those changes can often favor later entrants who are unencumbered by earlier designs. Consider the following cases.

Cott pioneered sugar-free soft drinks in 1947. It met with only limited success. In the 1950s, Kirsch, a Brooklyn-based bottler, introduced its "No-Cal" line aimed primarily at diabetics who could not consume sugar. It promoted its brand extensively and found that more than half of those who bought it were not diabetics but consumers trying to lose weight. In 1957 the industry sold 7.5 million cases of sugar-free soft drinks. In 1962 Royal Crown introduced Diet Rite Cola. It reduced the price to that of regular soft drinks, placed it in standard returnable bottles, and positioned the product against sugared soft drinks. It worked. The timing, the form, and the customers were right. Sales in 1962 doubled to 50 million cases. Other regional competitors jumped into the market. Coke and Pepsi held back, doubting the potential of the product. A year later, they revised their forecasts and entered with Tab and Patio Cola, respectively. Patio Cola failed and was quickly replaced with Diet Pepsi. With huge advertising expenditures, the two firms quickly dominated the market. No matter how innovative, Royal Crown could not hope to compete with the advertising and distribution advantages of Coke and Pepsi.

The pattern was repeated with low-calorie beer. Rheingold's Gablingers and Meister Brau's Lite Beer were regional brewers that pioneered this market in the 1960s with little success. The beers did not taste very good and, more important, were advertised as "diet" beers to men who were embarrassed to ask for the product at the local pub. Miller Brewing bought the Meister Brau's Lite name, stripped off the manufacturer's name, and introduced Miller Lite in 1975. Learning from previous failures, it improved the beer's taste and adopted an advertising campaign that overcame previous image problems. Diet beer was nowhere to be found. Now masculine athletes asked for the beer that did not fill them up. It worked, although Anheuser-Busch's Bud Light, an even later entrant, is a relentless competitor, keeping up the advertising pressure after failing with Natural Light.

Videocassette recorders followed a similar pattern. Throughout the 1960s many firms attempted entry, without success. Sony entered the consumer market with Betamax in 1975 by stressing the time-shifting capabilities of the product but lost its position to an even later entrant, Matsushita.

Pioneering, like the forecasts on which it is ultimately based, carries many risks. Almost every aspect of an emerging market is unknown, making the pitfalls for a pioneer plentiful. First, there is the problem of identification. Many growth opportunities turn out to be no such thing. Instead, they are traps for cash, management attention, and other resources that, in hindsight, could have been deployed in more profitable endeavors. Many pioneers end up pursuing false leads that later entrants are able to avoid.

Second, markets that do grow often do so in unexpected ways. The ultimate use of the product, its design, the primary customers, and even the structure of the industry are unknown in the beginning, and they often change dramatically as the market evolves. Furthermore, the task of educating and persuading first-time buyers to purchase falls squarely on the shoulders of the pioneer. It is an expensive proposition that pays off only if the pioneer can later fend off subsequent entrants.

Besides that, the pioneer must be willing to commit a great deal of up-front money for R&D, identification of key product attributes, plant construction, and consumer education. It is all done with the hope that the benefits of being the first to market will outweigh the risks of sailing in uncharted waters.

The key benefit of entering after the pioneer accrues from the experience of the pioneer. Specifically, once the potential of a growth market is proved, later entrants rely on some combination of (1) marketing clout, (2) product enhancement, and (3) low-cost production to negate the advantages of pioneering. It may not be any less expensive, but it is less risky and relies less on forecasts.

Expertise in marketing, and a lot of money to implement it, can often overcome the advantages of pioneering. In a sense, later entrants can buy what they were unable to foresee. That is especially true if a well-heeled firm is entering a market pioneered by a poor upstart. Not only did Coke and Pepsi have little trouble displacing Royal Crown's Diet Rite Cola in the mid-1960s, but Royal Crown's caffeine-free soda faced a similar fate a decade later. It is difficult to beat firms that have a headlock on distribution.

A strategy of entering "second but better" can also work for later entrants. Since the ultimate form that an innovation will take can rarely be predicted, it is unlikely that the pioneer will enter the market with a product that cannot be improved upon.

In crock pots, for example, it may be as simple as making a pot with a removable crock that can be placed in the dishwasher.

Low-cost production can also displace pioneers who had greater foresight. That is especially true when a dominant form of the product has emerged and the product has become standardized. When the product design has stopped changing radically, a later entrant can capitalize on the low-cost production of "me-too" products and capture a large share of a proven growth market. Foreign competitors with lower cost structures have often succeeded in this way, to the chagrin of domestic pioneers.

The standardization of many products in consumer electronics has pushed many earlier entrants to specialty segments where margins are higher, and the chances for differentiation are greater. For example, hand-held calculators and digital watches are products that were introduced by domestic producers but later dominated by later lower-cost foreign competitors.

Personal computers followed a similar pattern. IBM owned the market until the product stopped changing. Once the market settled on a specific form, low-cost foreign clones invaded the market. Consumers, less worried that they would be stuck with an orphan format, decided in droves to buy on price.

The pattern was repeated in microwave ovens. Domestic manufacturers were besieged by imports once the market opened up. Although Raytheon's Amana pursued the market for twenty years, lower-cost producers from the Pacific Basin have stolen a large share of it. These Johnny-come-lately entrants were less concerned with market forecasting. They knew that rushing to market would not preclude their gaining a hefty share of it. Amana's twenty-year lead turned out to be worth little when confronted with price competition by savvy copiers.

Perpetual Innovation

Another alternative to long-term forecasts is to innovate frequently, and on all fronts, in the hope that some percentage of the innovations will ultimately serve a large market. It also minimizes the chances that competitors will stumble across a huge success before you do. Perpetual innovation is a strategy that inoculates against poor forecasts by pursuing many products simultaneously. It is a strategy based on action rather than deliberate study.

The entire running shoe industry offers a good example of perpetual innovation. New models are introduced constantly and have a short life span. Old models have been on the market for a year, maybe. Shoes that incorporate all sorts of new technologies, such as gas bubbles and gel pads, for all sorts of runners and runner's maladies, are introduced. Some, such as Nike's Air Max, turn into huge successes, while others linger in warehouses. Rather than predict which styles will be successful and which will not, companies in this industry introduce many new products and end up with a few large successes.

Casio, the watch company, follows a similar strategy. New models of sports watches are introduced at a rapid rate. There are watches for swimmers, divers, moto-cross racers, joggers, runners, and racers of every persuasion. Each sport is offered a long line of watches, not a single watch. Some prove successful and some fail. The company tests the market with myriad entries rather than try to predict the market's response to a few new products chosen after careful study. It stresses action and eschews long, detailed studies.

If a firm wishes to pursue a more proactive strategy of innovation, it must also be willing to engage in creative destruction of its currently profitable product lines. The firm must make way for the innovations that may ultimately make those product lines obsolete. Many firms are reluctant to do so, even when it is clear that they have no other choice.

As a previous chapter detailed, market leaders often miss major market opportunities in their own backyards. They become complacent about the future. They mistakenly assume that their current products will stay at the forefront of the market forever.

One reason why firms shy away from revolutionary new products is that they are fearful of cannibalizing current product lines. Why should a firm take a chance on an unproven product when they have the lion's share of a proven one?

It is a tough decision, but it is not one that can be ignored. Eventually, firms must move with the new technology.

A strategy of perpetual innovation is based on three component parts. Each is described below.

Start Small

Most of the forecasts examined in this book proved far too optimistic. Partly, that was because the people who made the forecasts believed that the innovations on which their forecasts were based would go on to serve a huge market. It was often projected that the innovations would change our lives greatly. But in most instances the innovations never made it to commercialization or served only a small market where the benefits it provided matched the price that had to be charged for it.

Overly optimistic forecasts that call for spectacular wonders go hand in hand with large-scale new product development efforts. Those processes seek to discover huge market successes. Tom Peters refers to them as the search for "home runs." But, he observes, most of the innovations that have gone on to become huge successes have come from more modest starts. Most of the forecasts that failed in this study were predicting a home run. Most struck out in turn.

More conservative forecasts have a damping effect on grandiose strategies. Forecasts that call for smaller markets serve to lower expectations. They also lower the "downside" risk that comes with the inevitable occurrence of unexpected events.

The advice derived from the examination of failed forecasts here is very consistent with the advice offered by Tom Peters. More conservative forecasts argue that a firm should start small and seek to find a small but profitable niche in the market. That gives them the chance to expand as the potential for the market becomes more apparent.

Most important, the call to start small is more in tune with preparedness for the vagaries of the future. It is not possible to foresee where a market is headed, how large it will be, or what types of products and strategies will succeed. Starting small is a far better choice.

Photovoltaics offers a prime example of the difference between the search for a small but profitable niche and the "home run" mentality.

Solar-powered photovoltaic cells have not proved cost competitive with more traditional fuel sources. They have also been resistant to the dramatic cost declines necessary to penetrate large markets. Declines in fuel prices have worsened their competitive position. Those factors could not have been predicted.

In the United States, research and development for photovoltaics is largely supported by the federal government. But Americans have become bearish on the prospects for solar energy in general and photovoltaics in particular. Government expenditures for R&D are declining. Few markets seem feasible.

Many of the projects funded by the government were for massive schemes to build utility-sized photovoltaic projects. The effort was clearly to conquer energy dependence with massive government funding for R&D. We were going to belt one out of the park with that level of effort. Profitability was not the prime mover. In fact, business interest subsided with the level of government funding. Business interest seemed more oriented toward getting grants than finding profits in photovoltaics. After all that effort, there were still few commercial applications to be had.

Japanese interest in the technology, however, remains strong and oriented in a different direction. The Japanese have pursued a much smaller market, perfecting photovoltaics for watches, calculators, and other low-energy products. They have found a successful beachhead from which to expand to other viable markets as they emerge, if in fact they ever do.

Whatever happens to photovoltaics, the Japanese are far better positioned to take advantage of it than are the Americans. They are ready to proceed with small incremental moves when the time comes. Until then they must satisfy themselves with the current market.

Research on robots tells the same tale. American efforts are often complex, highly theoretical, and impractical. We try to make robots that replicate the highly coordinated movements of the humand hand. The detail is incredible, if unreliable. Japanese robots are jury-rigged to perform simple, mundane business tasks reliably.

The lesson to be learned is that massive projects to conquer markets rarely meet expectations. Forecasts predicated on such conquests are equally likely to fail. Study after study has confirmed this fundamental proposition.

Take Lots of Tries

Hand in hand with the advice to start small goes the advice to pursue many small projects simultaneously. Tom Peters, pursuing the baseball analogy, advises business to take lots of "at bats," trying to hit singles in product planning, rather than slug for the home run.[11] The record of growth market forecasts examined in this book strongly supports his advice.

Predicting huge growth markets often leads to strikeouts. Pursuing a project on a grand scale in the belief that it will grow quickly and surely often leads to disappointment. Opportunities often come from unexpected sources. What is expected is usually not what occurs.

The logic behind "lots of times at bat" is consistent with what we know about technological forecasting. It is also similar to the multiple coverage strategy that derives from multiple scenarios. In it a firm strives to follow many developments at once, spending a little on a lot of different projects. The goal is to keep your finger in as many pies as possible. A multiple coverage strategy is the antithesis of placing all your eggs in one basket. (Metaphors are many in descriptions of alternatives to forecasting.)

Many firms that followed rather than led were pursuing a multiple coverage strategy. They were funding many small, limited R&D projects. When the future became apparent, they were not caught totally off guard. They might not have been the first to market, but they were usually prepared for most developments in their field.

IBM offers a good example. Although it introduced a personal computer after Apple, Tandy, and a host of upstarts, it had been working on prototypes of small computers for at least a decade. The business press actually showed pictures of its early machines, which look odd in hindsight, and rely on tape rather than disk drives, but it was working toward a machine that eventually would help it enter the market for PCs. When it entered, it entered big.

Enter Big

The risk in growth market forecasting lies at the beginning, not once market growth is under way. Forecasts have failed far more often than firms that entered later. Many firms have used their vast resources, or a competitive advantage in distribution, marketing muscle, or other special competence, to catch up and surpass their risk-taking competitors. Usually this entails lots of money. It is expensive to dominate a growth market, or even to build a dominant position in it. But it is possible if a firm enters big.

Many growth markets have been dominated by competitors who entered "big" once the potential of the market became apparent. In doing so, they were generally able to surpass earlier entrants or to stave off later attempts to steal share.

There are many examples of this pattern. Coke and Pepsi failed to recognize the potential of diet soft drinks until just about every other firm in the industry was in the market. One marketing manager noted in the early 1960s, "This thing is pulled by advertising and most dollars are still going into regular soft drinks."[12] He was right and he was wrong. Advertising clout, along with distribution, does move those markets, but the battle did move to diet soft drinks. Not to worry. Even though his implied forecast was for little interest in diet soft drinks, he knew that no other firm could match the marketing prowess of Coke and Pepsi, not by a mile. When the time came, they entered big and blew away the innovators.

Gaining or defending the dominant position in a growth market will decimate profts for many years. Miller's Lite beer and Perrier's bottled water were provided with such extensive promotional support, over such a long time period, that neither entry turned a profit until well into the 1980s. They were able to maintain market leadership, but at a very high price. Sony spent heavily on Betamax, the largest expenditure in the firm's history.

Influence the Outcome

A final way to circumvent long-term growth market forecasting is to influence the outcome. Specifically, the following factors seem most important.

Setting Standards of Uniformity

Setting standards can have a profound effect on the commercial success of technological products. It does so by lowering risks to consumers. A standardized product ensures that consumers will not end up with an "orphan" product made obsolete by a subsequent design. Reducing customer uncertainty increases the likelihood of early purchase and speeds diffusion. A recent study initiated by Barry Rosen looked at the issue of product standardization.[13]

Contrast the case of the compact disk player, which grew quickly, with four-speaker quadraphonic systems, which did not. In the early 1970s it was widely believed that quadraphonic systems would replace two-speaker stereos in much the same way that stereo systems had replaced single-speaker hi-fi systems a decade earlier. It did not happen. Consumers were confronted with a bewildering array of competing and incompatible products, each of which required records produced specially for that standard. There were true four-channel systems, phased-sound systems, and systems that merely modified the sound of existing systems. Most consumers were reluctant to bet on a single standard. Sales were slow, and quadraphonics were withdrawn within a few years of their initial entry.

Manufacturers of compact disks tried a different strategy. They purposely cooperated to set an industry format that would avoid consumer confusion and foster industry growth. They were successful. The compact disk player became one of the most successful consumer products of the mid-1980s. In this case the firms involved were able to influence the accuracy of the underlying forecasts. By reducing risks to consumers, they were able to boost the market's prospects.

There are myriad examples of technological products that did not take off until a uniform standard was set for them. Household electricity is one. Today, the U.S. system is standardized on alternating current of 110 volts/60 cycles. In the 1880s, however, when the technology was new, there was vigorous competition between George Westinghouse, who favored alternating current, and Thomas Edison, who favored direct current. Household electricity did not diffuse widely until the AC standard was set.

Setting standards is most important for innovations that use complementary products. Stereos, for example, need stereo records, compact disk players require compact disks, computers need software, and VCRs require tapes to play on them. In each instance, products produced in other industries are required to use the innovation.

The problem is that firms that produce the complementary products are often reluctant to do so until an installed base of consumers has purchased the innovation. But consumers are reluctant to purchase until a supply of complementary products is available to make their purchase worthwhile. Clearly, new products that depend on complementary products are in a far more precarious position than those that do not.

Standards are also important when an innovation connects to other products. Local area networks, plug-compatible computer hardware, telephone systems, and other products that require interconnections benefit greatly from a standard format.

Standardization is also important when many users bring to an innovation a set of learned practices and expectations. Typewriter keyboards, for example, must follow the historical, albeit inefficient, "qwerty" standard. Typewriters with the superior "dvorak" keyboard are unacceptable, given the skills of existing typists and their reluctance to adopt a new standard. Consequently, forecasts for the growth of innovations that break with an existing standard are likely to be mistaken.

Standardization is least important for innovations that work independently and are not dependent on the common practices of users. Consequently, forecasts for stand-alone innovations have a better chance at success, all other things being equal. Fewer obstacles stand in their way.

Standards get set one way or another. They can be purposely planned or set through competitive market processes. Governments can set standards by government fiat, through their purchasing power, or by sugggestion. Firms in an industry can cooperate in setting standards for the good of the entire industry. Governments can either sanction industry cooperation or play an active role in the setting of technological standards.

Current trends suggest that coalitions are becoming more acceptable to both government policy in the United States and the general populace. That is largely a response to competition from Europe and Japan, where coalitions have long been accepted and encouraged. While we were breaking up large, powerful companies, foreign governments encouraged them.

Still, in the United States firms that cooperate run the risk of being charged with collusion and restraint of trade. In fact, the threat of antitrust suits alone has been enough to limit cooperative technical ventures between U.S. firms.

A leading manufacturer can often set standards single-handedly through the force of its market presence. IBM, for example, set the MS-DOS standard for personal computers, even though it entered the market years later than other producers.

Whatever the mechanism by which standards are set, setting standards is a way in which a firm can take some of the control back from an uncertain environment. By setting standards on a new technological product, firms can increase the odds that forecasts calling for that product to spawn a huge growth market will come true.

Developing the Necessary Infrastructure

Some innovations have the unfortunate distinction of requiring not only the development of the product itself but an entire infrastructure. Electricity, electricity generation, electric power lines, and electric appliances are examples. As a result, forecasts for those innovations should be more pessimistic than for innovations that do not carry such an onerous burden. At best, the diffusion of such innovations will take longer. At worst, they will never occur.

Firms can shift the odds of success by confronting the problem directly. They must recognize that the infrastructure must be created before the innovation can succeed. Thomas Edison, for example, arranged financing for power companies to supply electricity, obtained the rights to string electric distribution wires and the advanced "three-wire" distribution systems, as well as inventing the incandescent electric light bulb. Edison created not only the product but an entire industry of supporting products.

Ensuring a Supply of Complementary Products

The success of some innovations depends on the existence of complementary products. Complementary products are required to use the innovation.

The problem is that firms that produce the complementary

products are reluctant to do so until an installed base of consumers has purchased the innovation, while consumers are reluctant to purchase until a supply of complementary products is available to make their purchase worthwhile. Clearly, new products that depend on complementary products are in a far more precarious position than those that did not.

VCRs were hindered for nearly a decade by the dilemma of complimentary products. Throughout the 1960s, hordes of firms signaled their intention to enter the consumer market for VCRs but were scared off by the risks. None of them could find a way to have movies available for consumers along with the machines themselves. Many of the efforts to enter the market were a coalition of a "machine" company with a "movie" company. CBS attempted entry in the early 1970s. Its strategy was to enter the consumer market with prerecorded movies and a player. It withdrew in 1971 after losing tens of millions of dollars. AVCO entered in 1972 with a massive promotional campaign. Sears carried its $1,350 product, and Montgomery-Ward carried a "me-too" entry made by Admiral TV. AVCO withdrew the following year after losing $60 million.

Sony succeeded with a strategy that creatively overcame the problem with complementary products. It endered the consumer market with Betamax in 1975. It concluded that previous entries had failed because they relied on prerecorded tapes that were not widely available. Sony's strategy emphasized "off-the-air" recording and backed it up with the largest promotional campaign in the firm's history. It followed rather than led, started small—gaining experience in industrial markets—handled the problem of complementary products, and entered big once the potential became clear. As a result, it dominated the market for many years before losing its position to an even later entrant, Matsushita.

Lowering Prices

Some products simply cost too much when they are first introduced. Fortunately, the price of many products can be driven down as volume declines, and production efficiencies are realized. But for some products declines are much smaller than is necessary for widespread adoption of the product. In such instances, frims can speed diffusion by finding other ways to lower prices. Consider the initial steep price of copiers.

In the beginning almost no one believed photocopiers has potential. High costs suggested the potential market was only a few thousand. One study showed that the market for photocopying machines was limited: carbon paper was cheap, and few companies used enough copies to justify a machine. The machine was too expensive—it cost $4,000. One forecast predicted that a thousand machines could be sold to replace high-end offset printing—ironically, a segment Xerox has yet to penetrate significantly.

Xerox sidestepped high prices by leasing machines instead of selling them. Copy quality and convenience were emphasized. Steadily, Xerox copies supplanted carbon copies. Its strategy for effectively reducing the price of the machine put the price in balance with benefits.

Facsimile machines lingered for decades until technological advances boosted benefits and allowed price declines to spawn a larger market. Only now, after many false starts, has the market for facsimile machines exploded. The balance between price and performance has been struck.

In sum, firms can take many actions to minimize the effects of mistaken forecasts. Those actions, combined with the commonsense rules for constructing better forecasts presented in the previous chapter, can only improve on the historical record. Even the most cynical or skeptical reader must agree that it certainly cannot hurt.

Assume That the Future Will Be Similar to the Present

So much has been said and written about the accelerating rate of change in today's world that the idea passes largely unchallenged. It is as if by being stated so many times, by so many, the idea must be true. The idea itself has become a cliché. To challenge it is to be controversial.

It also has great intuitive appeal. From today's perspective things do seem to be changing faster. Everyday observations seems to prove the point. But there have been no devastating wars, famines, or massive forced dislocations (at least in the developed world). Furthermore, we still live in houses made of traditional materials (not plastic), and wear cotton and wool clothes (not paper or plastic). An objective comparison reveals that the things we do today are not that different from the things that were done yesterday.

The notion of accelerating change has been mentioned since at least as far back as the 1930s. But it was most widely espoused in response to the 1960s in popular books that foresaw "future shocks" and even entire new epochs in the history of mankind. I am skeptical and have strange beliefs. I suspect that tomorrow's markets will be remarkably similar to today's. There will be changes to be sure, but they will be no more drastic that those of the past. I also believe that those changes will be more disruptive to people who expect accelerating rates of change than to those who expect fewer and slower changes. While they aim at moving targets, others shoot down stationary targets.

The hypothesis of accelerating change is just not supported by the empirical evidence of past forecasts. Most of the forecasts examined in this book overshot their targets by a mile. They expected a world that would change much faster and more radically than it actually did. If our world is changing so quickly, why didn't the forecasts underguess more often? Common sense suggests that in a world of accelerating change, forecasting errors would have been less skewed in one direction. There would have been more cases where the world changed faster than the forecasts anticipated.

A more likely explanation is that our expectations of change have accelerated—promoted by the widespread acceptance of the mistaken idea that we live in a world characterized by accelerating change. Consequently, forecasts based upon those expectations have been grossly mistaken. Actual rates of change have been far more modest.

The evidence strongly implies that we should temper our forecasts, especially technological forecasts, to postulate smaller changes than we have in the past. It has been the smaller change forecasts that have been most successful. In the future, the same is likely to hold true. Our lives in the future are likely to be remarkably similar to our lives today. Tastes and styles will change, and discoveries will make life more convenient, but we will not be doing things radically different. Those schemes are for those who see visions of sugarplums dancing in their heads. And, like past forecasts that presumed accelerating change, they are likely to be very wrong.

Notes

CHAPTER 1. Introduction

1. Consumer Reports, *"I'll Buy That: 50 Small Wonders and Big Deals that Revolutionized the Lives of Consumers"* (Mount Vernon, N.Y.: Consumers Union, 1986).

CHAPTER 2. Overvaluations of Technological Wonder

1. "New Products: Setting a Timetable," *Business Week*, May 27, 1967, p. 52+.
2. Harper Q. North and Donald L. Pyke, "Probes of the Technological Future," *Harvard Business Review*, 47, no. 3, (May–June 1969): 68–76.
3. "Corporation Issues Major Forecast of Future Development," *Futurist*, October 1967, pp. 68–69.
4. The 1966 *Wall Street Journal* "Shape of the Future" series included the following articles: Alfred L. Malabre, "Population Rise to Pose Problems, but Efforts Made to Ease Impact," December 6, pp. 1 and 23; Thomas J. Bray, "Meeting World's Need for Food Will Require a Big Jump in Output," December 13, pp. 1 and 23; Stanley Penn, "Computers Will Bring Problems Along with Their Many Benefits," December 20, pp. 1 and 19; William D. Hartley, "Huge Nuclear Facilities Will Help the U.S. Meet Surging Power Demand," December 27, pp. 1 and 10; Richard P. Cooke, "Airline that Will Top 4,000 MPH Is Expected Before End of Century," December 29, pp. 1 and 13. Parenthetical citations in text refer to articles bearing the appropriate date.
5. The 1976 *Wall Street Journal* "The Future Revisited" series included the following articles: Alfred L. Malabre, "U.S. Unlikely to Be as Big—or as Rich—as Analysts Thought," March 15, pp. 1 and 14; Joan Libman and Herbert Lawson, "The Family Troubled by Changing Mores, Still Likely to Thrive," March 18, pp. 1 and 27; Barry Kramer, "Wiser Way of Living,

Not Dramatic Cures, Seen as Key to Health," March 22, pp. 1 and 19; Joseph M. Winski, "By 2000, Prevention of Starvation May Be Chief Global Concern," March 25, pp. 1 and 23; James Tanner, "No Crippling Shortage of Energy Expected, but Cost Will Be High," March 29, pp. 1 and 23; Todd Fandell and Charles Camp, "Transportation in 2000 to Rely on Equipment Much Like Today's," April 1, pp. 1 and 24; Roger Ricklefs, "Cities May Flourish in South and West, Decline in Northeast," April 6, pp. 1 and 32; R. Martin and R. J. McCartney, "Education's Big Boom Is Ending, but Studies to Get More Diverse," April 8, pp. 1 and 27; Jonathan Spivak, "Population of World Growing Faster than Experts Anticipated," April 12, pp. 1 and 13; Richard J. Levine, "Conventional Warfare Changing Faster than the Experts Predicted," April 15, pp. 1 and 23.

6. Herman Kahn and Anthony J. Wiener, *The Year 2000: A Framework for Speculation on the Next Thirty-Three Years* (New York: Macmillan, 1967).

7. "In Your Future: Robot Slaves, Instant Knowledge, Sea Farms . . . ," *U.S. News and World Report*, April 10, 1967, pp. 112–13.

8. "Opinion Poll Results: Future Advances—Readers Tell When They Should Be Expected," *Industrial Research*, May 1968, p. 45.

9. P. Michael Sinclair, "Looking Forward: 10 Years Ahead," *Industrial Research*, January 1969, p. 68.

10. The 1967 *Fortune* "The U.S. Economy in a New Era" series included the following articles: William Bowen, "The U.S. Economy Enters a New Era," March, pp. 110+; Lawrence Mayer, "II. Why the U.S. Population Isn't Exploding," April, pp. 162+; Morris Cohen, "III. The Coming Boom in Housing," May, pp. 135+; Jeremy Main, "IV. A Slow Getaway for the Auto Market," June, pp. 111+; Lawrence Mayer, "V. Home Goods: But What Will They Think of Next?" August, pp. 114–140.

11. Lawrence Lessing, "Where the Industries of the Seventies Will Come from," *Fortune*, January 1967, pp. 96–192.

12. "The New World of Superconductivity," *Business Week*, April 6, 1987, p. 94.

13. "Our Life Has Changed," *Business Week*, April 6, 1987, p. 94.

14. Lessing, "Industries of Seventies," p. 99.

15. "Technologies for the '80s," *Business Week*, July 6, 1981, p. 48.

16. "High Technology: Wave of the Future or a Market Flash in the Pan," *Business Week*, November 10, 1980, p. 96.

17. "Dentistry's Brave New World," *Business Week*, March 2, 1968, pp. 58+.

18. Isaac Asimov, *Futuredays: A Nineteenth-Century Vision of the Year 2000* (New York: Henry Holt, 1986).

19. George Wise, "The Accuracy of Technological Forecasts 1890–1940," *Futures*, 8, no. 5: 411–19.

20. S. Corum Gilfillian, "The Prediction of Inventions," in *Technological Trends and National Policy* (Washington, D.C.: Government Printing Office, 1937), pp. 15–23.

21. Steven P. Schnaars and Conrad Berenson, "Growth Market Forecasting Revisited: A Look Back at a Look Forward," *California Management Review*, 28, no. 4 (Summer 1986): 71–88.

21. Frank Trippett, "Why Forecasters Flubbed the '70s," *Time* January 21, 1980, pp. 91–92.

CHAPTER 3. Life at Home in the Future

1. Michael de Courcy Hinds, "Habitat: A Lonely Leader in Housing," *New York Times*, July 26, 1987, section 8, pp. 1–20.

2. The 1967 *Wall Street Journal* series "Shape of the Future" included the following articles: Jonathan Spivak, "Manned Mars Landing, Moon Base Are Seen As Likely Space Feats," January 6, pp. 1 and 14; Jerry E. Bishop, "Satellites Will Make Global Picture Phones and Facsimile Possible," January 16, pp. 1 and 12; Laurence O'Donnell, "Concern over Pollution and Safety Will Force Major Changes in Cars," January 23, pp. 1 and 10; Herbert Lawson, "Electronic Wizardry Will Transform Life in Tomorrow's Homes," February 6, pp. 1 and 13; Richard Martin, "Education Will Become a Lifelong Process, Lean on Electronic Aids," February 13, pp. 1 and 22; William Carley, "Medical Gains to Slash Heart, Cancer Deaths, Reduce Birth Defects," February 21, pp. 1 and 16; Frederick Taylor, "U.S. Builds Capacity for Both Nuclear War, Vietnam-size Conflicts," February 27, pp. 1 and 8. Parenthetical page references relate to article identified in text.

3. Augustus B. Kinzel, "The Face of Tomorrow," *Public Utilities Fortnightly*, May 11, 1967, pp. 37–38.

4. See Mayer (Chapter 2, note 10), p. 115.

5. "Some of the 500's New Products," *Fortune*, May 1971, pp. 153–57.

6. "60 and the 60s: The Decade of Man in Space," *Newsweek*, December 14, 1959, p. 25.

7. Michael Rogers, "Home, Smart Home," *Newsweek*, November 3, 1986, p. 58.

8. See Lessing (Chapter 2, note 11), p. 191.

CHAPTER 4. A Bias Toward Optimism

1. William Avison and Gwynn Nettler, "World Views and Crystal Balls," *Futures*, 8, no. 1 (February 1976): 413–14.

2. Tyzoon T. Tyebjee, "Behavioral Biases in New Product Forecasting," *In-*

ternational Journal of Forecasting, special issue on "Forecasting in Marketing," 3, no. 3/4 (1987): pp. 393–404.

3. Nigel Calder, *The World in 1984,* Vol. 1 (Baltimore: Penguin Books, 1964).

4. Nigel Calder, *1984 and Beyond,* (New York: Viking Press, 1983), p. 47.

5. Everett M. Rogers, *Diffusion of Innovations,* 3d edition, (New York: Free Press, 1983), p. 7.

6. Allan Nevins, "The U.S. in 1970: Three Forecasts," *New York Times,* May 17, 1959, p. 76.

7. See Malabre, (Chapter 2, note 4).

8. See Malabre (Chapter 2, note 5).

9. See Martin and McCartney (Chapter 2, note 5), p. 1.

10. See Hartley (Chapter 2, note 4).

11. "The Future That Never Came," *Forbes,* 122 (July 10, 1978): 51–52.

12. Sam Love, "Whatever Became of the Predicted Effortless World?" *Smithsonian,* 10 (November 10, 1979): 86–92.

13. "Anniversary Edition of I.I.I. Publication Views Life in 1980s," *The National Underwriter,* 74 (February 13, 1970): 8.

14. Everette Gardner and Ed McKenzie, "Forecasting Trends in Time-Series," *Management Science,* 31 (October 1985): 1237–46.

15. Steven P. Schnaars, "A Comparison of Extrapolation Models on Yearly Sales Forecasts," *International Journal of Forecasting,* 2 (1986): 71–85.

16. "For Videotex, the Big Time Is Still a Long Way Off," *Business Week,* January 14, 1985, pp. 128–33.

17. "Two Videotex Heavyweights Quit," *Business Week,* March 31, 1986, pp. 31–32.

18. Andrew Pollack, "Ruling May Not Aid Videotex," *New York Times,* September 15, 1987, pp. D1 and D6.

19. "CB: The Competition Heats Up," *Dun's Review,* May 1976, pp. 53–55.

20. "Getting Mail by Phone," *Business Week,* September 28, 1968, pp. 158+.

CHAPTER 5. The Zeitgeist

1. Irvin Molotsky, "No Sign of Slowing Down as Jet Engine Marks 50th," *New York Times,* April 14, 1987, p. A19.

2. "A Think Tank that Helps Companies Plan," *Business Week,* August 25, 1973, pp. 70–71.

3. "Report to Management: How Industry Will Find World in 1986," *The Iron Age,* January 5, 1967, p. 23.

4. Richard E. Rustin, "The Future Is Now, So Where Is the 3-D TV and Those 4 Cars?" *Wall Street Journal*, October 10, 1979, p. 31.

5. "Down to the Sea by Jet Power," *Business Week*, January 22, 1966, pp. 152+.

6. "Nowadays Only the Exceptional Sells Well," *Business Week*, April 8, 1961, pp. 64–68.

7. "Japan Lifts Its Targets," *Business Week*, June 17, 1961, pp. 131–34.

8. "L.A. to Tokyo in Two Hours," *Newsweek*, December 16, 1985, p. 66.

9. Rustin, "Future Is Now."

10. See Spirak (Chapter 3, note 2), p. 1.

11. See Hartley (Chapter 2, note 4), p. 1.

12. Joe Catalano, "A Time of Decline for U.S. Shipbuilding," *Newsday*, August 23, 1987, p. 82.

13. William J. Broad, "Reactors in Space: U.S. Project Advances," *New York Times*, October 6, 1987, p. C12.

14. "Brainier Robots for Brawny Jobs," *Business Week*, January 28, 1961, pp. 81–82.

15. "AEC Is Refining Nuclear Earth-Excavation for '67 Project, Perhaps New Canal Later," *Wall Street Journal*, January 6, 1965, p. 2.

16. See Love (Chapter 4, note 12), p. 90.

17. See "60 and the 60s" (Chapter 3, note 6), p. 88.

18. See Mayer, "Home Goods" (Chapter 2, note 10), p. 117.

19. See Lawson (Chapter 3, note 2).

20. See "Some of 500s New Products" (Chapter 3, note 5), p. 156.

21. Theodore Levitt, "Marketing Myopia," *Harvard Business Review*, 38 (July–August 1960): 46.

22. Malcolm Browne, "Sound Is Shaped into a Dazzling Tool with Many Uses," *New York Times*, February 9, 1988, pp. C1 and C13.

CHAPTER 6. Price-Performance Failures

1. "Dehydrated Food Looks Ahead," *Business Week*, October 15, 1960, pp. 77+.

2. "A Confusing Start for Quadraphonics," *Business Week*, November 11, 1972, pp. 72+.

3. "Goodyear: Making Sales Forecasts Come True," *Business Week*, December 16, 1972, pp. 50+.

4. Paul Ingrassia, "Tire Makers Are Turning to Technology to Improve Gas Mileage, Wear, Traction," *Wall Street Journal*, March 24, 1982, section 2, p. 29.

5. Joseph Pereira, "Future Interactive Toys Promise to Give Viewers More Control over TV Screens," *Wall Street Journal*, November 23, 1987, p. 29.

6. John Holusha, "G.M.'s High-Tech Visions of Sales," *New York Times*, January 6, 1988, pp. D1–D6.

7. John Holusha, "Advances: Infrared Rays May Improve Night Driving," *New York Times*, October 10, 1987, p. D8.

8. "Is the Computer-Phone Market Ready to Explode?" *Business Week*, August 13, 1984, pp. 101–2.

9. "Computerphones: The Heavyweights Could Start Bells Ringing," *Business Week*, March 4, 1985, pp. 110–11.

10. Paul Gardner, "On the Decline and Demise of Professional Soccer," *New York Times*, February 17, 1985, p. 2.

11. See "Corporation Issues' Major Forecast" (Chapter 2, note 3).

12. Frank P. Davidson, *Macro: A Clear Vision of How Science and Technology Will Shape Our Future* (New York: William Morrow, 1983), p. 19.

13. "NASA's Next Stop in Space," *Newsweek*, January 19, 1987, pp. 52–53.

14. "Heavy Betting on a Light Fiber," *Business Week*, January 31, 1970, p. 33.

15. "Tire that Makes Air Old-Fashioned," *Business Week*, April 6, 1968, pp. 114+.

16. N. R. Kleinfield, "An Eternal Lightbulb in Every Socket," *New York Times*, March 16, 1986, p. 11.

17. "A Second Generation for Plastic Paper," *Business Week*, April 15, 1972, p. 108.

18. Irwin Dorros, "Picturephone," *The Bell Laboratories Record*, 47, no. 1 (May–June 1969): 136–41.

19. "We're Working to Give You One Like This" (AT&T picture telephone advertisement), *Business Week*, May 27, 1967, p. 59.

20. "Picturephones: Unfullfilled Promise," *U.S. News and World Report*, June 14, 1976, p. 73.

21. "A Long Look Ahead," *Bell Telephone Magazine*, 51, no. 1 (January–February 1972): 1–7.

22. John Naisbitt, *Megatrends: Ten New Directions Transforming Our Lives* (New York: Warner Books, 1982).

23. James Tanner, "Food from Fuel: Protein Made from Oil May Swell Food Supply," *Wall Street Journal*, June 9, 1967, p. 6.

24. John Holusha, "Diesels Seem to Have Run out of Steam," *New York Times*, December 30, 1984, Section 4, p. E2.

25. "Damn the Smog, Full Speed Ahead," *Forbes*, February 1, 1971, p. 36.

26. "Opinion Poll Results: Automakers Are Holding Back Development of Steam Power," *Industrial Research*, October 1968, p. 109.

27. "An Iffy Future for the Steam Car," *Business Week*, February 9, 1974, p. 72.

28. "The Rotary-Engine Car Is Catching On," *Business Week*, July 10, 1971, p. 20.

29. "The Little Cars Are Hotter than Ever," *Business Week*, April 11, 1970, p. 20.

30. See Love (Chapter 4, note 12).

31. See O'Donnell (Chapter 3, note 2).

32. "No-Frills Food: New Power for the Supermarkets," *Business Week*, March 23, 1981, pp. 70–80.

CHAPTER 7. Demographic, Social, and Political Trends

1. See Malabre (Chapter 2, note 4), p. 1.

2. See Ricklefs (Chapter 2, note 5), p. 32.

3. See Nevin (Chapter 4, note 6), p. 77.

4. James Bylin, "1970: What the Prophets Saw," *Wall Street Journal*, December 22, 1969, p. 12.

5. "A Friendly Rivalry Goes Up in Smoke," *Business Week*, June 20, 1970, p. 33.

6. "Social Security's Galloping Surplus," *Business Week*, October 18, 1969, pp. 41+.

7. Charles E. Silberman, "Technology Is Knocking at the Schoolhouse Door," *Fortune*, August 1966, p. 120.

8. "The Coming Boom in Solar Energy," *Business Week*, October 9, 1978, p. 88.

CHAPTER 8. Successful Forecasts

1. "Old Age Gets into Politics," *Business Week*, February 13, 1960, pp. 62+.

2. "Biggest Market Ever Coming Up," *Business Week*, May 13, 1961, p. 147.

3. "Population Growth: Will Markets Develop as Hoped?" *Business Week*, May 15, 1965, pp. 32–34.

4. "Our Affluent Economy Will Be Bursting at the Seams by '85: Brown," *Advertising Age*, October 12, 1970, pp. 1 and 81.

5. Burton G. Malkiel, *A Random Walk down Wall Street*, (New York: W. W. Norton, 1973), p. 246.

6. "A Hot Year for Microwave Ovens," *Business Week*, September 8, 1980, p. 33.

7. "Campbell Soup: Cooking Up a Separate Dish for Each Consumer Group," *Business Week*, November 21, 1983, pp. 102–3.

8. "Americans Change," *Business Week*, February 20, 1978, pp. 64–70.

9. "The New Rich South: Frontier for Growth," *Business Week*, September 6, 1972, p. 30.

10. Stanley E. Cohen, "Population Boom Will Build Markets, but It'll Also Breed Problems Galore," *Advertising Age*, February 13, 1967, pp. 4 and 108.

11. Stephen B. Packer, "Population Growth and Market Forecasting," *Financial Analysts Journal*, March–April 1966, p. 18.

12. "The Graying of the Soft Drink Industry," *Business Week*, May 23, 1977, pp. 68–72.

13. "Miller's Fast Growth Upsets the Beer Industry," *Business Week*, November 8, 1976, pp. 58–67.

14. "Mirror, Mirror on the Wall," *Business Week*, May 7, 1966, pp. 150+.

15. "Cash Drawers that Talk Computer," *Business Week*, August 29, 1970, p. 66.

16. "A New Kind of Flight Plan for Small Freight," *Business Week*, November 3, 1973, p. 68.

17. Gregory Weber, "Will Paper Cans Catch On?" *Newsday*, August 13, 1986, p. 9.

18. See Spivak (Chapter 3, note 2).

19. See Mayer, "Home Goods" (Chapter 2, note 10).

20. "How to Create Your Own TV Show," *Business Week*, January 7, 1967, p. 128.

21. "Ready-Mix Woos the Drinker," *Business Week*, September 17, 1960, p. 150+.

22. "Bottled Water Sales Begin to Sparkle," *Business Week*, November 7, 1970, pp. 44+.

23. "Stride Rite: Still Trying to Use Keds to Grow out of Children's Shoes," *Business Week*, August 9, 1982, pp. 51+.

24. "Plotting Time-Cost Schedule," *Business Week*, February 17, 1962, pp. 81+.

25. "Electronics Goes Microminiature," *Fortune*, August 1962, pp. 99+.

26. "Where IBM Looks for New Growth," *Business Week*, June 15, 1968, pp. 88+.

27. "Microcomputers Aim at a Huge New Market," *Business Week*, May 12, 1973, pp. 80+.

28. "Fuel Crisis in the Making," *Business Week*, July 29, 1972, p. 64.

CHAPTER 9. Some Conclusions About Growth Markets

1. "Classrooms Get Set for Airborne Television," *Business Week*, January 28, 1961, p. 111.

2. Laurie Hays, "Du Pont's Difficulties in Selling Kevlar Show Hurdles of Innovation," *Wall Street Journal*, September 29, 1987, p. 1.

3. Kirk Johnson, "Technology's Martyrs: The Slide Rule," *New York Times*, January 3, 1987, section 3, p. F17.

4. Hays, "Du Pont's Difficulties," p. 1.

5. Martin Levine, "Tall Troubles for Big-Screen Pioneer," *Newsday*, June 22, 1987, part III, p. 5.

6. William J. Abernathy and James M. Utterback, "Patterns of Industrial Innovation," *Technology Review*, June–July 1978, pp. 41–47.

7. John Jewkes, David Sawers, and Richard Stillerman, *The Sources of Invention* (New York: St. Martin's Press, 1959), p. 237.

8. Ralph Biggadike, "The Risky Business of Diversification," *Harvard Business Review*, 57 (May–June 1979): 103–11.

9. Derek F. Abell, "Strategic Windows," *Journal of Marketing*, 42 (July 1978): 21–26.

CHAPTER 10. Improving the Accuracy of Growth Market Forecasts

1. "Industry Warms Up to Microwaves," *Business Week*, March 13, 1965, pp. 152–56.

2. "The Jogging-Shoe Race Heats Up," *Business Week*, April 9, 1979, pp. 124+.

3. Alexis N. Sommers and Ferdinand F. Leimkuhler, "A Non-Demographic Factor V/STOL Prediction Model," *Technological Forecasting and Social Change*, 1 (1969): 170.

4. Richard E. Neustadt and Ernest R. May, *Thinking in Time: The Uses of History for Decision Makers* (New York: Free Press, 1986).

5. William Ascher, *Forecasting: An Appraisal for Policy Makers and Planners* (Baltimore: John Hopkins Press, 1978).

CHAPTER 11. Strategic Alternatives to Forecasting

1. "Goodrich: Something Very Drastic . . . Had to Be Done," *Business Week*, July 1, 1985, p. 27.

2. Harold E. Klein and Robert E. Linneman, "The Use of Scenarios in Cor-

porate Planning: Eight Case Histories," *Long Range Planning*, 14 (October 1981): 69–77.

3. "Piercing Future Fog in the Executive Suite," *Business Week*, April 28, 1975, pp. 46–52.

4. *Ibid.*

5. "The Doctor Performing ARCO's Radical Surgery," *Business Week*, June 3, 1985, pp. 64+.

6. Steven Schnaars and Martin Topol, "The Use of Multiple Scenarios in Sales Forecasting: An Empirical Test," *International Journal of Forecasting*, special issue on Forecasting in Marketing, 3, nos. 3–4 (1987): 405–19.

7. Theodore Levitt, "Exploit the Product Life Cycle," *Harvard Business Review*, 43 (November–December 1965): 81–94.

8. Theodore Levitt, "Innovative Imitation," *Harvard Business Review*, 44, September–October 1966): 63–70.

9. "Coke's Big Marketing Blitz," *Business Week*, May 30, 1983, pp. 58–64.

10. C. Merle Crawford, *New Products Management*, 2d ed., (Homewood, Ill.: Richard D. Irwin, 1987).

11. Tom Peters, *The New Masters of Excellence*, audiocassette programs (Chicago: Nightingale-Conant Corp., 1986).

12. "Sales Bubble for Diet Drinks," *Business Week*, June 27, 1964, pp. 88–90.

13. Barry Rosen, Steven Schnaars, and David Shani, "A Comparison of Approaches for Setting Standards for Technological Products, *Journal of Product and Innovation Management*, vol. 5, no. 2 (June 1988).

Index

197